Endorsements

"Finally, a book that frames the evangelist within the whole Christian story and the holistic mission of the church. This is the book I will give to people in my church when they wa[...] vision for telling and living the Christia[...]

"Finally. A book...I can give to people in my church as an inspiration to participate with God in mission, and as a resource with tools to actually do it. What's more, I can give it to pastors and leaders across the country, because it is theologically sound, and challenges our current paradigms."

Cam Roxburgh, DMin
Senior pastor, national director (Forge Canada)
British Columbia, Canada

"Set within the larger framework of God's unfolding story of redemption, Grant articulates what it means for us to live credibly and speak seamlessly about the good news of Jesus. This book is a crucial resource for the church in these turbulent times."

Daron Boyd Brown
Senior pastor, author
Tennessee, USA

"Zweigle has given us a significant contribution to the consideration of evangelism in the contemporary context that is both practical and theologically reflective. I highly recommend this book to all who are interested in being and proclaiming the gospel in a postmodern world."

Ron Benefiel, PhD
Dean, Point Loma Nazarene University
California, USA

"Zweigle's passion...is contagious. This insightful book will instill in anyone a deeper desire to worship God and invite others do the same."

Dick Eugenio, PhD
Associate pastor, assistant professor, author
Manila, Philippines

"For those trained in transactional evangelism strategies that seem increasingly out of place in a post-Christian world, Zweigle's real-life examples and suggestions are life-giving and encouraging. I will ask every pastor under my oversight to spend time with this book."

Jeren Rowell, DMin
Nazarene district superintendent, author
Kansas, USA

"*Worship, Wonder, and Way* is written with a balanced combination of academic training, extensive pastoral experience, and practical application. Zweigle mixes a blend of proven Wesleyan principles with an understanding of contemporary culture. This book will challenge you to a new adventure of missional living and discipleship journey!"

David A. Busic, DD
Nazarene general superintendent, author
Kansas, USA

"For anyone wondering what a healthy Christian witness can look like, how it can function, or the possibilities it can embody in a post-Christian culture, let the hope and faithfulness found in this book be your guide."

Timothy R. Gaines, PhD
Co-pastor, co-author
California, USA

"If you have ever wrestled with the idea of evangelism, this is the book for you. Grant Zweigle challenges the inadequate conceptions of this vital aspect of the kingdom of God. This wonderful resource will relieve you of unnecessary guilt and empower you for the churchly task of evangelism."

Jesse C. Middendorf, DMin
Executive director, Center for Pastoral Leadership
Nazarene Theological Seminary, Missouri, USA

"Grant Zweigle is a passionate and practical witness of Jesus. This book is a delightful read for anyone with an interest in the relevance of methods and practices of evangelism."

Eugénio Duarte, MBA, MA, DD
Nazarene general superintendent
Kansas, USA

"Grant Zweigle's book is an engaging and powerful resource, inviting the church to rediscover and rekindle a passion for evangelism in accordance with the Word of God. This book will revolutionize the way we have understood evangelism and will offer a new and much-needed perspective for the accomplishment of the call to make Christlike disciples in the twenty-first century".

Fili Chambo, PhD
Regional director, Church of the Nazarene
Johannesburg, South Africa

"Grant takes the fear out of evangelism. His approach invites all believers into the journey of evangelism. I highly recommend this book to all believers who are serious about their call to share Christ."

Scott Rainey, DMin
CIS Field strategy coordinator, former Nazarene pastor
Kyiv, Ukraine

"Grant Zweigle offers his readers a reminder of what it means to testify. If you are uncertain about evangelism, read on! I was encouraged, challenged, and equipped as I read, and you will be too."

Olivia Metcalf
University chaplain, author, public speaker
Idaho, USA

"Has evangelism gone out of style? Grant Zweigle takes us on a thoughtful journey where he explains the current landscape. No, evangelism hasn't gone out of style; it just may look different! Zweigle provides excellent handles on the ways in which each of us can thoughtfully be engaged in sharing Christ with those we encounter. This is an important read for everyone growing as faithful disciples."

Carla Sunberg, PhD
NTS president, professor, author
Missouri, USA

"Zweigle's stories of transformation illustrate the heart of the gospel. He provides a cross-cultural approach to witness... This book is a must-read for church leaders...in a diverse and changing world."

Mark A. Maddix, PhD
Dean, professor (Northwest Nazarene University)
Idaho, USA

Worship, Wonder, and Way

Reimagining Evangelism
as Missional Practice

Grant Zweigle

BEACON HILL PRESS
OF KANSAS CITY

Copyright © 2015 by Grant Zweigle

Beacon Hill Press of Kansas City
PO Box 419527
Kansas City, MO 64141

978-0-8341-3525-3

Printed in the
United States of America

Cover design: Sherwin Schwartzrock
Interior design: Sharon Page

Library of Congress Control Number: 2015931269

The internet addresses, email addresses, and phone numbers in this book are accurate at the time of publication. They are provided as a resource. Beacon Hill Press does not endorse them or vouch for their content or permanence.

10 9 8 7 6 5 4 3 2 1

Contents

 Introduction

On my twenty-fourth birthday, I experienced what some people might call a "spiritual awakening." It happened in the middle of an ordinary worship service in an ordinary church of the Nazarene in southwestern Idaho. I don't remember any particular thing the preacher said or that the worship team sang that precipitated this experience. But as the pastor prayed that morning, I discerned a voice speaking clearly to the inner depth of my being saying, "Grant, repent of your sin and come follow me." It was Jesus.

I first heard the name *Jesus* when I was a young child. I learned about Jesus from my mom and dad, as well as from Sunday school teachers and preachers in the churches I attended throughout my youth. I learned about Jesus in the Christian college I graduated from. Jesus was a familiar and friendly figure to me. I believed in Jesus. And I knew that calling people to repent and follow him was one of the things Jesus did. But, up to that point in my life, I can't say I had ever experienced him calling *me* to turn from *my* sin and follow him in such a clear, direct, and personal way.

The next morning I was at my pastor's doorstep, asking if he would help me become a follower of Jesus. I knew enough about Jesus to know that following him is not a solitary pursuit. I knew I needed guides for this journey. And I knew enough about Jesus to know that he would want me to guide others on the journey as well. I also recognized that I didn't know how to do that.

Over the next several months I met with my pastor, Orv Halley, on a weekly basis. He prayed with me and taught me from Scripture. He listened to my joys and struggles as I adapted to a life of Christian discipleship. He shared his heart for the nations with me, and spoke excitedly of his dream for our little church in southwestern Idaho to send a team to plant a church in a closed-access country in central Asia.

Another young man in the church met with us. This man would eventually move his family halfway around the world to start a church among an unreached people group in central Asia.

Orv's love for God, his love of people, and his enthusiasm for the mission of God in the world were infectious. It did not surprise him at all that Jesus would speak to a young man like me, calling me to follow Jesus and join Jesus's redemptive mission in the world. Orv had an understanding of the gospel that was wide and expansive, inclusive and generous. Orv's understanding of God's mission in the world was rooted in the Old Testament, in places like the creation story; in God's calling and choosing of Abraham to be a blessing to all the peoples of the earth; in Psalms that spoke of God's heart for the nations; and in Israel's calling to be a light to all the nations of the earth. Orv believed that the Holy Spirit was active in the world, seeking young women and men just like me, desiring to enfold us into the triune life and love of God and send us out, on mission, for the life of the world.

As he discerned the gifts and graces God had given me, Orv began to give me little assignments in the life and mission of our local church. One day, several months after we began meeting, Orv asked me to share the gospel with Shelly, a woman who was on the margins of our church. Shelly was someone Orv believed showed signs of spiritual openness. I had never shared the gospel before, with anyone, so I asked him to help me. I could sense by the hesitation in his response that he wasn't exactly sure how to guide me.

First, he pulled a copy of *Evangelism Explosion* off his shelf and suggested I read it. Recognizing that this might be too much for me to digest in a short amount of time, he offered me a small gospel tract called "Life Can Have True Meaning" as a guide. As I flipped through this tract in preparation for my meeting with Shelly, I found the way it talked about the gospel to be quite small in comparison with the more robust and compelling vision Orv shared with me in our weekly meetings and in his preaching and teaching. Perhaps this was the reason for his hesitation?

The next day I met Shelly in the church office. Opening the tract on the coffee table between us, I talked while she listened, following the point-by-point explanation of the gospel found in the tract. At the end of my talk, I asked Shelly if she would like to accept Jesus Christ as her personal Savior. Much to my surprise, Shelly said yes. Following the instructions in the back of the tract, I led her in the prayer printed there and, afterward, assured Shelly that she had been saved.

> Have you ever been trained to share the gospel with someone? Did you learn a particular method or plan of salvation? How do you feel about that method today? Does it still make sense? Is it still effective? Or have you needed to tweak it?

It was a wonderful, yet, I'll admit, somewhat confusing experience. There was nothing in the tract about following Jesus or joining God's redemptive mission in the world. Nothing about God's heart for the nations and God's desire to enfold all people into God's triune love. I'm not sure what sort of transformation was taking place in Shelly's life, but something happened inside me. My interest in evangelism ignited.

Several months later, when filling out my application to attend Nazarene Theological Seminary, I ticked the box next to the word *evangelism*. Within a short time I received an enthusiastic call from Dr. Charles "Chic" Shaver, professor of evangelism at

NTS, who heard about my interest in evangelism from the registrar. By the time our conversation ended, Chic had invited me to join him and his wife, Nancy, on a series of revival meetings he was holding in Omaha, Nebraska. By the time I returned from that trip, Chic had convinced me to enroll in his personal evangelism course. That course changed the trajectory of my life. By the end of my first semester at NTS, I switched from my declared degree of MA in Christian thought and history to master of divinity with an emphasis in evangelism. Later that year I became Chic's faculty assistant, and by the next year, I was serving as assistant pastor of evangelism at Kansas City First Church of the Nazarene and managing director of the Chic Shaver Center for Evangelism.

It was at Kansas City First Church that I met my wife-to-be, Aisling, whose mother had received a visit from First Church's personal evangelism team, led by Pastor Chic Shaver, when Aisling was just a little girl.

Chic's passion for evangelism was infectious, and I was inspired. But, as I continued my seminary education, I could sense that other students and certain faculty members were not enthusiastic about the methodology used in the evangelism courses, particularly *Evangelism Explosion*. As I grew in my own understanding of church history, ecclesiology, soteriology, biblical studies, and Wesleyan theology, I began to see why certain aspects of the methodology taught in my evangelism courses were not congruent with other aspects of the seminary curriculum.

How does your understanding of Scripture or church tradition affect your practices of evangelism? Are there tensions between your theological worldview and certain practices of evangelism that you have seen or participated in?

But at the same time, I was a firsthand witness to the fruit of Chic's ministry, and my appreciation of him and growing friendship with him kept me from becoming overly critical or dismissingly cynical. Instead, I chose an appreciative posture, in order to learn as much as I could from a man who was clearly blessed with the gift of evangelism and had a deep love and concern for people, while resolving at the same time to study and develop practices of evangelism that were congruent with my growing understanding of a Wesleyan biblical-theological perspective.

That opportunity came with my first assignment after graduating from seminary. In 2000, I was appointed pastor of the Seattle Beacon Hill Church of the Nazarene, a small, multicultural church in an urban neighborhood of Seattle. The Beacon Hill church was labeled a mission church on the district. The forty or so regular attenders represented at least a dozen different nationalities. I moved from pastoring in one of the wealthiest neighborhoods in the United States to one of the poorest. The church in Kansas City had been religiously, politically, socially, and economically homogenous. The church in Seattle was diverse, with attenders who had Orthodox, Catholic, and various strands of Protestant backgrounds; lawyers, single mothers on welfare; Democrats, Republicans, Independents; citizens, immigrants, refugees, undocumented persons. My context in urban Seattle was significantly different from suburban Kansas City.

Outside the church, the Pacific Northwest is a place where skepticism, cynicism, and criticism characterize people's attitude toward Christianity and the church. My new neighbors were "happy pagans" with little interest in or felt need of the church. The diversity of our community put me in regular contact with people from other faith traditions, as well as immigrants from countries like China, whose outlook on life was totally different from mine. Many of these immigrants had an Eastern spiritual worldview, as opposed to my Western materialist worldview. Yet they did not believe in God, in contrast to the dominant theistic belief system of the West.

All of this created a challenge for me. My evangelism training at NTS assumed common cultural ground with the people I had been equipped to share the gospel with. The gospel I was taught was a series of narrow propositions that assumed the hearer's familiarity with the wider Christian story. My own experience of conversion was built on familiarity with words like *repentance,* and my prior knowledge of and familiarity with Jesus. When I heard Jesus calling me to follow him, I recognized the voice. My new friends and neighbors did not know this voice. I now pastored among a people who did not share my culture or my worldview, and who were unfamiliar with the basic trajectory of the Christian story. Some were people who had never heard the name *Jesus* before.

In Seattle, I was first introduced to the vision of the missional church: the church as a people who are sent by God into the world, for the life of the world. As we began to shift our ministry programming toward engaging the community and creating a hospitable, welcoming community of worship, we experienced growth and renewal as we walked with people on the journey of becoming followers of Jesus.

In 2005 we moved from Seattle, Washington, to Vancouver, British Columbia, Canada, to pastor the Vancouver First Church of the Nazarene. Much like our church in Seattle, the church in Vancouver was multicultural, located in an urban neighborhood where two-thirds of our neighbors spoke a first language other than English. Seattle and Vancouver share a similar cultural outlook, but it became clear rather quickly that my new Canadian friends and neighbors in Vancouver were not only skeptical, cynical, and critical of Christianity like those in Seattle; they also vacillated between the poles of total indifference and outright hostility toward Christians and the church.

The propositional approach to evangelism I had been taught in seminary, using logic, argumentation, and rhetorical moves that would "seal the deal" are viewed in Vancouver as manipulative, disrespectful, and antithetical to Canadian multicultural values where faith is relegated to the private, interior space of people's lives, and not to be shared with others in a way intended to change hearts and minds or secure converts. As a result, my neighbors were on their guard against any perceived attempt to proselytize.

One evening over dinner at a neighbor's house, my neighbor looked at me with what can only be described as an expression of bemused amazement and said, "I never imagined I'd ever have a pastor over to my house for dinner." In another conversation, a neighbor grilled me about what my church believed for an hour and a half on a frigid elementary school playground. At the end of the conversation, he was still hostile toward the Christian church but said, in a manner I assume he meant as a compliment, that "at least [I wasn't] one of those religious fundamentalists."

How would you feel if you learned that a friend from a different religion or denomination viewed you as lost and in need of saving?

In the context of ministry in both Seattle and Vancouver, I began to develop a theology and practice of evangelism that are congruent with a Wesleyan, biblical perspective but also appropriate in my unique context. It was also during this time that I began to delve deeper into what has come to be known as missional theology, the origins of which can be traced to Lesslie Newbigin, who, upon returning to his home country of England after serving as a missionary in India, realized he needed to apply the same tools of contextual analysis and missiological reflection to the practice of ministry in England that he had in India. The context had changed, and so, too, did the methods of evangelism.

In this book, I set out to share some of my reflections on a theology and practice of the witness and evangelism of the local church that I have found useful in my congregational contexts in Kansas City, Missouri; Seattle, Washington; and Vancouver, British Columbia. Much of the content of this book was originally conceived as a series of teaching sermons developed for my church in Vancouver as part of a pastoral research project for my doctor of ministry degree. Good preaching needs to be informed by a deep well of theological study and biblical reflection, but it also needs to be relatable and understandable to the person in the pew, folding chair, barstool, or whatever people are sitting on when they receive it. This book will be successful only if it is understandable to the average reader but also opens avenues for deeper reflection by those who are more theologically attuned.

Scattered throughout the book are reflection questions for personal or group use. My hope is that this book will be a resource for local churches seeking to reimagine evangelism as a missional practice of their churches. The questions are designed to help congregants and congregations apply the content of the book to their unique contexts.

The theological vision for this book is shaped by a set of core convictions that I have come to hold about evangelism and the mission of the church. This theological vision did not originate inside of me; rather, it is a synthesis of the reading and reflection I did for my doctoral degree. As a pastor, I worked out this theological vision in the context of congregational ministry. This is not armchair theology; it was developed and tested in the trenches.

In their introduction to *The Study of Evangelism: Exploring a Missional Practice of the Church*, Paul Chilcote and Laceye Warner offer six propositions concerning evangelism that strongly influence the theological vision of this book. Through my pastoral experience and doctoral research, I've developed, adapted, and added to these propositions for my own use. In quick summation, they are laid out thus: First, evangelism is a vital part of something larger than itself, *the mission of God*. Second, evangelism has discipleship to Jesus as its primary *telos*, or goal. Third, evangelism is an invitation to participate in the kingdom of God. Fourth, evangelism is designed to provide a good start in the process of conversion. Fifth, evangelism is a missional practice of the whole people of God together. Sixth, my additional proposition, evangelism must be inherently personal. And seventh, evangelism is inescapably contextual.[1]

As any working pastor knows, time is a precious commodity. And the time it took to complete my doctoral degree and write this book was often borrowed from family, friends, and my congregation. I want to thank my wife, Aisling, and my sons, Graiden and Abram, for their support and patience during the research and writing of this book. My parents, Gary and Eleanor Zweigle, as well as my wife's family, have been tremendously supportive along the way. I am blessed with a family who desire to be part of God's redemptive mission in the world, and who support and encourage me to develop the gifts God has given me for this mission. Thank you!

I am also grateful to the congregations of Kansas City First Church of the Nazarene, Seattle Beacon Hill Church of the Nazarene, and Vancouver First Church of the Nazarene for the privilege of being their pastor and for everything they taught me about what it means to be witnesses together. I love pastoring. My love of pastoring is directly related to the people I have pastored. It has been a joy to pastor these wonderful people!

> ◗●◗●◗●◗●◗●◗●◗●
>
> Who encourages you to develop the gifts and graces God has given you? What are your favorite ways of participating in God's redemptive mission in the world?

Since beginning this book, I have completed a doctor of ministry at Nazarene Theological Seminary, and have accepted the position of dean of students at Asia-Pacific Nazarene Theological Seminary in Manila, Philippines. I am grateful for the fine schools of the Church of the Nazarene, and for opportunities to both learn from and serve our schools. Moving from North America to the Asia-Pacific region is providing me new opportunities to explore and learn about evangelism in a different context.

I am also indebted to ministry colleagues who have read portions of this book and provided valuable feedback along the way. I learn from others, and it would be dangerous for me to try to list all the wonderful women and men who have given input into the theological and practical vision that inform this book. You know who you are! Thank you!

I appreciate the fine women and men at Nazarene Publishing House who encouraged me to write and who kept this book alive through some difficult and challenging days. A special thank you to Audra Marvin for her many suggestions to improve the original manuscript.

Finally, I cannot express enough gratitude to the two most significant mentors in my life: Orv Halley and Chic Shaver. Both of these men invested long hours in me and taught me how to pastor with a global vision that is at the same time attentive to the persons around me who are not yet following Jesus and need a guide for the journey to Jesus. Orv completed his journey and is now with the Lord. Chic continues to witness with boundless enthusiasm and energy.

My life is not my own. I am eternally grateful to Jesus for calling and choosing me to be his follower. That Sunday when Jesus called me to follow him forever changed the trajectory of my life. Through Jesus I came to know a Father who loves not only me but the whole world, and through Jesus I have received the Spirit, who equips and empowers me to serve others in Jesus's name. Through Jesus I have indeed learned that life can have true meaning. All glory be to God the Father, Son, and Holy Spirit.

1 · Mission as Witness

Acts 1:8: But you will receive power when the Holy Spirit comes on you; and you will be my witnesses in Jerusalem, and in all Judea and Samaria, and to the ends of the earth.

Driving home on a sunny day in beautiful Vancouver, British Columbia, Canada, I stopped at a traffic light and noticed a sign tacked to a telephone pole just outside the passenger side window. It said: "Witnesses needed." I leaned over the empty seat to get a closer look and read that there had been an accident at that very intersection. It gave the date and time of the accident and asked for anyone who had seen the accident to call the phone number listed on the sign. It is such a simple request: *Witnesses needed*. But it's a weighty request as well. Without a witness, the victim's ability to resolve the claim with the insurance company is significantly diminished. Without a witness, the circumstances surrounding that event will never be fully revealed. Without a witness, the truth of what occurred at that intersection will never be known.

The operation of our whole legal system hinges on the willingness of credible witnesses to report what they have seen and heard. A witness often appears in the courtroom as part of a trial. "This witness is in every way one of the people, but...is placed on the stand because of two credentials: the witness has seen something [that is of importance to the outcome of the trial], and the witness is willing to tell the truth about it—the whole truth and nothing but the truth."[1]

But not every act of witness takes place in the courtroom. Every day we tell truthful stories to one another, bearing witness to things we've seen, heard, felt, learned, and experienced. We bear witness to truth in a variety of ways. Some people are natural storytellers who take you on a journey in their retellings. Others prefer to speak directly and get straight to the point.

A good novelist writes stories that witness to the truth of human experience through the use of fictional characters. A director instructs actors to perform in such a way that truthfully bears witness to a story written by another. A symphony bears witness to a piece of music by performing it truthfully before an audience—interpreting, but not deviating too far from the notes originally penned by the composer. Artists bear witness to the full scope of human experience through the media of paint or pencil, canvas or computer, stone or clay. Historians bear witness to the past by reconstructing events into a truthful timeline, discerning meaning by connecting pieces from the past. Scientists bear witness to the validity of their experiments by publishing their research in peer-reviewed scholarly journals.

What we know about life in this world, how we understand the past and present, and even what we expect of the future is constructed largely on the basis of witnesses. As a people, we are constantly adding to our understanding of the world we live in through the witness of those who are willing to tell the truth about a whole range of human experiences. So, too, is our knowledge of God based on witnesses who are willing to speak truthfully about the God who comes near, entering human history in both powerful and humble ways.

The people of ancient Israel—the sons and daughters of Abraham, Isaac, and Jacob—are the first to bear witness to the God we've come to know through the Bible as *YHWY*, the LORD, Creator of the heavens and the earth. They bear witness to the truth that the God who creates is also a God who calls and makes covenant promises. The LORD is a God who blesses and a God who sends. This God also liberates, rescues, saves, and redeems. The children of Israel personally experience the redeeming and liberating power of the LORD in the Exodus event. They write songs that truthfully sing the story of how God delivered them from the powers of Egypt. They tell this story to their children, and instruct them to pass it on to their children. It is important to the Israelites that every generation bear witness to the next generation of how the LORD delivered them from bondage and brought them into the promised land.

The tabernacle in the wilderness and, later, the temple in Jerusalem bear witness to the wondrous—and, at times, dangerous—presence of the LORD among the people. The law of Moses organizes the life of Israel in such a way that it bears witness to a way of living in the world that expresses the holiness, mercy, and justice of the LORD. And through the witness of prophets, priests, and kings, the word and way of the LORD are made known to the people of Israel and the nations. When the people fail to bear witness to the saving deeds of the LORD, they lose their identity as a people and are sent into exile, where they remember who they are and *whose* they are. Also in exile, the longing is cultivated for a faithful and righteous king to come and make Zion a place of healing for the nations.

Israel's vocation at this time, as a people chosen by God, is to bear witness to the truth of God among all the nations of the earth. "'You are my witnesses,' declares the LORD" in both Isaiah 43:10 and 43:12, "'that I am God;'" and in 43:13, "'Yes, and from ancient days I am he.'"

When Moses goes up Mount Sinai, the LORD says to him:

If you were to name a person in the Old Testament who witnesses God's saving, rescuing, or healing power, whom would you choose? Why? What makes this person a credible witness?

This is what you are to say to the descendants of Jacob and what you are to tell the people of Israel: "You yourselves have seen what I did to Egypt, and how I carried you on eagles' wings and brought you to myself. Now if you obey me fully and keep my covenant, then out of all nations you will be my treasured possession. Although the whole earth is mine, you will be for me a kingdom of priests and a holy nation."

Exodus 19:3b-6a

Reflecting on this scripture, Michael Goheen writes: "It is hard to overestimate the importance of these words for understanding the role and identity of Israel."[2] Goheen continues:

Israel is to embody God's creational intention for all humanity for the sake of the world, living in such a way as to draw the nations into covenant with God. Or, to use the later language of Isaiah, Israel is called to be 'a light to the nations' (Isa. 42:6 NASB).[3]

There is no question that when Jesus comes preaching and teaching in Galilee, he understands his mission as an extension of and fulfillment of Israel's missionary vocation. "I am the light of the world," Jesus says in John 8:12, "Whoever follows me will never walk in darkness, but will have the light of life." Israel is called to be a light to the nations. Jesus is the light of the world.

In Revelation 1:5, John calls Jesus "the faithful witness." Israel's witness is imperfect. Jesus's witness is perfect. The writer of Hebrews puts it this way:

In the past God spoke to our ancestors through the prophets at many times and in various ways, but in these last days he has spoken to us by his Son, whom he appointed heir of all things, and through whom also he made the universe. The Son is the radiance of God's glory and the exact representation of his being, sustaining all things by his powerful word.

Hebrews 1:1-3a

Jesus is the image of the invisible God. Jesus truly and fully embodies God's creational intent for every person. Through his life, death, resurrection, and ascension, Jesus witnesses to the presence and reality of the kingdom of God that is now open to everyone who will believe, enter, and receive. Jesus announces and embodies the good news that, through repentance and faith in him, all people everywhere are set free from the powers of darkness and death; forgiven from the guilt and healed from the scourge of sin; and wel-

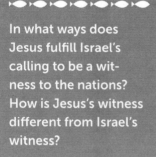

In what ways does Jesus fulfill Israel's calling to be a witness to the nations? How is Jesus's witness different from Israel's witness?

comed as children into the eternal-life-giving, loving fellowship of Father, Son, and Spirit. And to all of this, the Holy Spirit bears witness in the life of believers.

This is a story that needs to be told. It is a story that is for the life of the world. Jesus is the firstfruits of the new creation that is coming, the One who will reconcile the whole creation to God the Creator. The Christian church today is called to bear truthful witness to this story. The church bears witness to the wonderful truth that Jesus is the Messiah of Israel as well as the true Lord of the rest of the world; that, in Jesus, the reign of God has come near and is open and available to everyone who would receive; that the Creator God has reached into the world through the Son and the Spirit to enfold all people into God's rescuing, redeeming, and reconciling embrace, where we find life. Christians are sent to bear witness to their experience of and participation in the kingdom of God. The shorthand for this news is the gospel. Christians are a people whose life together in the world bears witness to the gospel.

Once upon a time, I was taught that the gospel was a set of logical propositions about God, humanity, sin, and salvation. I believed that witnessing to the gospel meant presenting these propositions in such a way that would convince a person to give assent to these facts by praying something that was called a "sinner's prayer." The problem with this approach is that this is not the way the Bible talks about the gospel. In its Old Testament usage, the word *gospel* was used for the good news that the reign of God—which sets captives free, brings exiles home, reconciles estranged peoples, and renews the whole creation—has come near. In the gospels of Matthew, Mark, Luke, and John, the gospel is the good news that the reign of God that the Old Testament prophets spoke about has finally arrived—in the person and work of Jesus Christ. The Gospels are the gospel!

According to Paul in 1 Corinthians 15:3-5, the gospel message includes the news "that Christ died for our sins according to the Scriptures, that he was buried, that he was raised on the third day according to the Scriptures, and that he appeared to Cephas [Peter], and then to the Twelve." But that is not the extent of it. Paul goes on to include in his telling of the gospel the good news that Jesus Christ now reigns as King, and will one day hand over the kingdom to God the Father after he has destroyed all dominion, authority, and power, including the power of death. The gospel, therefore, tells the whole story of Jesus and the rescuing, redeeming, and reconciling implications of his life, death, resurrection, ascension and imminent return for all people and all creation.

To bear witness to Jesus in our world today is to represent the whole story of Jesus for our whole world today. It is to speak and live the truth and nothing but the truth—the whole truth—about Jesus. This includes our witness to Jesus's ministry as a prophet greater than Moses, who graciously restores our knowledge of God's will for human life.[4] Jesus is the greatest teacher who ever lived. For example, in what has come to be known as the Sermon on the Mount, Jesus presents a compelling vision for a whole and integrated life. But it is also Jesus's prophetic ministry that calls us to consider the ways we fall short of the righteousness of the kingdom of God and our need for forgiveness and reconciliation and re-creation, the new birth made possibly by the power and presence of the Holy Spirit.

The whole truth about Jesus includes witnessing to Jesus as our great high priest. On the cross, Jesus took our sin upon himself, making full atonement for human sin. Through Christ, our priest, "we are each assured of the pardon of our sin, a pardon that initiates our restored relationship with God and that maintains us in that relationship."[5]

We live in a world that is vandalized by sin on a daily basis. We participate in this vandalism both willingly and unwillingly, burdening ourselves with guilt. And we are vandalized by the sin of others, which fills us with shame. Christ our priest atones for the guilt of sin and removes our shame, reconciling us with God and one another.

The whole truth about Jesus includes witnessing to Jesus as King, the Shepherd-King with healing in his wings, who makes all things new, restoring the image of God to those who have been reinstated in his favor and reigning at God's right hand until all things have been reconciled to him.[6] This includes the hope of Revelation 11:15, the day when "the kingdom of the world has become the kingdom of our Lord and of his Messiah, and he will reign for ever and ever." This is good news for the life of the world because it means the end of injustice, tyranny, pain, oppression, evil, sin, and death. Jesus is the King the world longs for, the King the whole creation groans for. Jesus is the one who makes all things new.

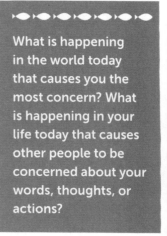

What is happening in the world today that causes you the most concern? What is happening in your life today that causes other people to be concerned about your words, thoughts, or actions?

Who will do this? Who will bear witness to this good news? Who will tell the truth, the whole truth, about Jesus and the reign of God? "You, church!" Jesus says in Acts 1:8. We will be Jesus's witnesses.

This, then, is our vocation, the mission of the Christian church, our mission of witness. But it is more than just a vocation, more than just a job, more than a task, more than a mission we are obligated to fulfill. Witness describes our very identity. Witness is who we are called and chosen to be. When Jesus says, "You will be my witnesses" in Acts 1:8, he is making a promise to his disciples, not giving them a command. And, by extension, he is making a promise to us today; we will be witnesses to Jesus Christ and the reign of God in our cities, neighborhoods, towns, and villages.

Of course, when Jesus first speaks these words to the apostles in Acts 1:8, he is speaking to those who have been physically with him from the very beginning of his public ministry, starting with John's baptism, throughout his ministry in Galilee, right through his rejection, passion, death, and resurrection, up to the time he returns to the Father in the ascension. He is speaking to those who have personally experienced the power of the kingdom of God through his miracles: restoring sight to the blind, healing lepers, rescuing people from demonic possession, raising the dead, forgiving sinners, preaching the good news to the poor.

But we, in the Christian church, are also those who have experienced the rescuing, redeeming, liberating, reconciling, and life-giving power of the kingdom of God in Jesus Christ. We can speak truthfully about times in our lives when we experienced release from the guilt and shame of sin; about times we have experienced the grace and love of God enfolding us into the mysterious, triune life of God in wondrous ways; about times we experienced God's help to love and serve others in ways contrary to our very nature; about how God worked in the lives of our families. For example, I can bear witness to how the LORD rescued my great-grandparents from the oppressive powers of communist Russia and delivered them safely to Canada. We witness to what we have learned and heard, and also to what we have personally experienced.

And we are not alone in our witness. The apostles are not the only witnesses to Jesus. In John 5:31-47, Jesus provides a list of other witnesses, including John the Baptist; the miracles he did; the Father, who says at Jesus's baptism: "You are my Son, whom I love; with you I am well pleased"; and the Scriptures, the entire Bible, bear witness to the truth about Jesus.

When you add these witnesses to the witness of the apostles and now—two thousand years later—the witness of the entire Christian church down through the ages, it is encouraging to know that we stand today among a great cloud of witnesses! We are not the first witnesses, and we will not be the last. And we are not asked to be lone, solitary voices crying out in the wilderness. We now stand shoulder to shoulder with all God's people through the ages, around the world, and gathered together in our local congregations. Together with all our sisters and brothers, we live as witnesses to Jesus and the rescuing, redeeming, and reconciling implications of his life for every person and the whole of creation.

So it is not just each one of us as individuals who are called to witness, but all of us together, as the body of Christ, as Christians. Everyone who has been captured by this story and the good news of God's reign in the Old and New Testaments; all who have looked to Jesus and found rescue, redemption, and reconciliation; all who have been baptized and have received the Holy Spirit; all who are filled with the love of God and desire to share God's love with others immediately become a part of the community of witnesses. We are all, together, by the power of the Holy Spirit, witnesses to Jesus Christ.

For a long time I imagined the Christian witness as sort of a solitary, lonely business. When I thought of an effective witness I thought of someone like Billy Graham, a towering figure standing alone behind a solitary pulpit, preaching about Jesus while the masses looked on. I thought of a witness as a solitary woman on a street corner, handing out tracts to those passing by, pleading with people to listen. I imagined a witness as a missionary couple, saying goodbye to family and friends, getting on an airplane and flying to some far-off land to tell people about Jesus. In fact, most of the time when I thought of witnessing, I thought about activities I was supposed to do apart from the Christian church, activities I would pursue away from the community of faith. I even, for a time, believed that the main role of the church was to equip me to be a witness and then send me out there on my own. I heard sermons that exhorted me, as an individual, to go out there and reach people for Jesus. Perhaps I mistakenly heard and understood this as an individual pursuit, or perhaps I sometimes heard misguided preaching. It certainly didn't come across to me that being a witness was designed to be a team effort.

Imagining witnessing as an individual activity, and believing that I bore an individual responsibility to witness to my friends, neighbors, coworkers, and unsaved family members often felt like a huge burden to bear. And I felt, at times, that if I wasn't individually pursuing opportunities to witness to unsaved individuals on my own, then somehow I was letting God down. I was failing. I wasn't doing what God expected me to do. I don't believe this anymore. And it is not what Acts 1:8 says.

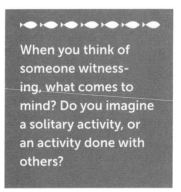

When you think of someone witnessing, what comes to mind? Do you imagine a solitary activity, or an activity done with others?

Jesus is speaking to his community of disciples. He is speaking to the women and men who have been with him, and who will now constitute the new community called by his name. This doesn't come across in the English language, but in the Greek, all the pronouns in Acts 1:8 are plural. *You all* will receive power, Jesus tells them. The Holy Spirit will come on *you all*. And *you all* will be my witnesses. All together now!

We never witness alone. We have the Holy Spirit, the third person of the Trinity, dwelling within us. "You will receive power when the Holy Spirit comes on you," Jesus promises. *You will receive, and you will be.* These are words of gift and promise. Our vocation, our mission of witness, is a gift of the Holy Spirit.

But, like every gift of the Spirit, the gift is given to us, but it is not exclusively for us. The gift is given *to* us *for* the world. Our witness is to be a public witness for the life of the world. The witness is for others; for those "in Jerusalem, and in all Judea and Samaria, and to the ends of the earth."

Jesus believes that the world needs a witness. Jesus believes that the world needs to taste and see and hear and experience the good news of the kingdom of God. The world needs to taste and see and hear and experience the gospel, the good news that God's reign in Christ has come near and is open and available for all who will turn and receive. Our vocation as a Christian congregation is, therefore, both a gift and a calling. A gift given to your church, for the life of your neighborhood.

Witnesses are needed in places like Seattle, Washington, and Vancouver, British Columbia, where I lived. Vancouver is a city in which the majority of people do not know or have forgotten the story of Jesus. A few years ago, a couple from China who were visiting professors at the University of British Columbia moved into our neighborhood and found our church. They came for our English Conversation Club and stuck around because of the warmth and hospitality of our congregation. During the English Conversation Club, the family heard about our hanging of the greens, when we decorate the sanctuary for Advent and Christmas. They showed up and asked if they could help. A woman in our church named Faye gave them the job of setting up the crèche, the manger scene. When they unpacked the figurines, they asked Faye, "Who are these people?" They did not know the story of Mary, Joseph, the shepherds, the wise men, and baby Jesus.

But it is not just immigrants from China who are unfamiliar with this story. The same month that Faye shared this story with me, she also told me of an experience she had when attending a Christmas program at another church in Vancouver. A stylish Canadian woman in her early thirties sat near Faye. She leaned over and asked, "Who do those figures on the table in front of the sanctuary represent?" She was asking about the crèche. She didn't know the story of Mary, Joseph, the shepherds, the wise men, and baby Jesus either! Witnesses are needed in Vancouver.

As we consider our witness in our cities, neighborhoods, towns, and villages today, I wonder if we can imagine the geographical scope of the witness that Jesus spoke to his apostles about in Acts 1:8—*in Jerusalem, all Judea and Samaria, and to the ends of the earth*—and apply it to the people in your local context, where your church has its home. Rather than using geographical proximity, perhaps we might think of being witnesses in Jerusalem as referring to our witness among those who are closest to the story of Jesus. Already among us are those to whom we bear witness. This is our witness to the beloved children of the Christian community. Our witness as a Christian community begins in our homes, in our children's Sunday school classrooms, in our sanctuary, at the dinner table, the small group, in service to others together, and through the normal routines of family and congregational life. Our children, youth, young adults, adults, and seniors are all constituents of our witness. We witness to one another all that we have seen and heard and know about Jesus. God loves all the children of the church, young and old. The beloved children of the Christian church are the first constituents of our witness— the first to whom our witness together is directed. Our Jerusalem is one another.

Expanding this metaphor, Judea and Samaria could refer to our witness among those who once were a part of the Christian community but have disconnected from the church for one reason or another. Walter Brueggemann calls these folks "forgetters." Forgetters are "insiders to the faith who have grown careless, weary, jaded, and cynical about the faith."[7] Beloved children of the community become forgetters for a variety of reasons. Sometimes there has been disagreement within the church that pushes people away. Others are unable to resolve the tough questions of faith and life and consequently disengage from the church. In North America, where Sunday worship is no longer protected as sacred time, forgetters are often those who just got too busy with life, work, sports, kids, recreation, shopping, etc., to pay attention to God.

Brueggemann points to affluence as a major contributor to "forgetfulness" in Israel's life in the Old Testament: "In a context of affluent prosperity, Israel would eventually forget its memory, scuttle the God of the memory, disregard the demands of that God and forfeit the joy of covenant with Yahweh."[8] Today only 2-3 percent of people in Vancouver are meaningfully connected to a local Christian church. Some of the 97 percent who are not connected to the church are "forgetters." There is some Christian memory. They might show up on Easter Sunday or ask us to baptize their children or perform their weddings. Most are indifferent to the church, while others have grown judgmental of or even outright hostile toward Christians.

The Christian church is to persevere in its witness among forgetters. God has not forgotten the forgetters. Forgetters are the lost son, the lost sheep, the lost coin of Luke 15. They are precious to our Father in heaven. We must continue to bear witness to the truth about Jesus in a world that has, in many ways, intentionally sought to push the church out of public life and seeks to relegate the Christian witness to the interior, private arena of individual souls. But we cannot keep quiet about what we have seen and heard! The gospel is for the whole world, not just for church folks. The gospel is good news for forgetters.

The third constituency for our witness is outsiders. If we apply the geographical scope of the church's witness to our local context, then "the ends of the earth" may refer to those in our cities, neighborhoods, towns, and villages who are truly outsiders to the story of Jesus. This would include those who have never received a true hearing of the story. It might include those who have never truly seen the gospel in action. It would include those whose parents never bothered to talk to them about spiritual things. It would include forgetters who have been away for so long that they have become outsiders.

In Jesus's parable of the great wedding banquet, which is all about the invitation to enter the kingdom of God, the insiders ignore the invitation to the feast. "Then the master told his servant, 'Go out to the roads and country lanes and compel them to come in, so that my house will be full'" (Luke 14:23). God sends God's servants to find and welcome outsiders into God's presence. Many immigrants to the United States and Canada are truly outsiders to the story of Jesus and the reign of God. They view Christianity as a Western religion. They associate Christianity with the worst forms of cultural imperialism.

God loves the outsider. God loves those who don't know that the kingdom is open to them. The kingdom of God is for outsiders. Witnesses are needed among outsiders. The ends of the earth have moved next door. The Master has prepared a lavish feast and wants them to come in! Is your church a witness among outsiders? Do the immigrants, strangers, and unchurched in your neighborhood know that they are welcome in your church or at your dinner table?

It is not easy to be a witness today. But it's never been easy. In the original Greek, the word for *witness* is *martyr*. In English, the word *martyr* refers to those who suffer or are put to death for their witness. We need to keep the words *witness* and *martyr* together so that we are not surprised by the difficulty and cost of being a witness to Jesus. But before Jesus revealed the cost, he promised his divine help in Acts 1:8: *You will receive power when the Holy Spirit comes on you; and you will be my witnesses in Jerusalem, and in all Judea and Samaria, and to the ends of the earth.* Be encouraged by this promise. God is fulfilling that promise today in the places you wor-

> ▶◆▶◆▶◆▶◆▶◆▶◆
>
> Have you ever been an outsider in any context, like immigrating to a new country or being a visitor to a church with unfamiliar traditions? What was that experience like? Who welcomed you? Who helped you fit in and understand your new surroundings?

ship, fellowship, raise families, work, play, and serve. You have received power. You have the Spirit. You are not alone. We are witnesses together.

2 ⟡ Our Witness of Worship

Acts 1:11: "Men of Galilee," they said, "why do you stand here looking into the sky? This same Jesus, who has been taken from you into heaven, will come back in the same way you have seen him go into heaven."

Quirks & Quarks is an award-winning, science-focused radio program of the Canadian Broadcasting Corporation. Every week the host interviews the people behind the latest discoveries in the physical and natural sciences. One Easter Sunday, after our worship service, I was driving home and tuned into a conversation between the host, Bob McDonald, and Dr. Justin Barrett, who is one of several researchers looking for the roots of religious belief in our brains. The question he is asking is this: *How and why are humans built, biologically, to believe in a divine being?*[1] Dr. Barrett suggests that humans have what one researcher calls "an agency detection device" hardwired in our brains, which is the ability to identify intentional beings in the environment around us.

Think of it this way. Have you ever been outside enjoying a walk when, suddenly, something that seems to be an alert signal goes off in your head, causing you to wonder: *What was that rustling noise?* In response, you find yourself searching for what you perceive to be the presence of another being around you. Or, you are at home alone at night and suddenly the question *Who's there?*

pops into your head when you hear a creak in the other room. Dr. Barrett believes this cognitive mechanism is highly tuned because detecting other intentional agents in the environment was extremely important to our ancestors. It was important to know whether that rustling noise was a friend or foe.

Humans are hardwired to stay tuned to the presence of other beings. We are social creatures, who are by nature attentive to others among us. This ability, according to some theories, explains the development of religion, when "the other" was perceived to be a divine being or spirit. At the end of the interview, host Bob McDonald asks Dr. Barrett if he is religious himself. Dr. Barrett answers, "I am," and explains that he is a Christian. Bob asks Dr. Barrett if his Christian faith is ever challenged by his research on the natural foundation of belief. Barrett responds:

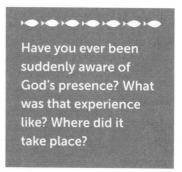

Have you ever been suddenly aware of God's presence? What was that experience like? Where did it take place?

> Not at all. From a Christian perspective, the notion that there is some kind of natural foundation for belief, something in our brains, something hardwired in our cognitive structure that makes us attentive to the divine other should not surprise us. God has created us with some kind of sense of the divine built in, and this would have to be worked out in some kind of cognitive architecture.[2]

We were created with the capacity to know and be known by God. We were created with the ability to be attentive to the presence of God in our midst, and to respond, turning our attention toward the divine presence.

In the story told in Genesis, the first man and woman are created with the ability to be attentive to the presence of the LORD in their midst. They are created for communion with God. They delight in God's presence until the day they yield to the temptation to stop trusting God's good intentions for them, and seek to develop life apart from God, lusting after the knowledge of good and evil without reference to God. After the woman and man reach out their hands, grasping and eating from the tree of the knowledge of good and evil, they hear a rustling noise in the garden. You might say that their agency detection device goes off! And they perceive that it is the LORD. Now they face the choice of whether to hide themselves or make themselves present to the LORD. For the first time they find themselves asking: *Is God a friend or foe?* With their knowledge of good and evil and the awareness that they have disregarded God's command, they are afraid, and they hide themselves.

People have either been turning toward the LORD or turning away from the LORD ever since. Yet people continue to want to find ways to respond to the divine presence that is rustling in the world. Down through the centuries, Christian theologians—from St. Augustine to Blaise Pascal to C. S. Lewis—have suggested that there is a God-shaped vacuum in the heart of every person, and it can never be filled by any created thing. Some who reject the God who created them create gods in their own image as a way to fill this "God-shaped hole" in their hearts. In the language of Romans 1:25, people "exchanged the truth about God for a lie, and worshiped and served created things rather than the Creator—who is forever praised."

The Bible is clear that God is lovingly concerned that people know and worship God alone. The God to whom the Bible bears witness is the God who creates and redeems; the God who saves and rescues; the God who calls and sends. The Scriptures are clear that this God, the God the apostle Paul first knows as the LORD God of Israel then comes to know as the God and Father of our Lord Jesus Christ, is forever praised. Though many in our world today have turned away from God and no longer worship their Creator, God is forever praised. Day after day, the creatures "in heaven and on earth and under the earth and on the sea, and all that is in them" continue to praise God, "saying: To him who sits on the throne and to the Lamb be praise and honor and glory and power, for ever and ever" (Revelation 5:13).

Whenever and wherever Christians gather for worship, we join this chorus of praise, lifting our voices together with creation and all the saints down through the ages, bearing witness through our worship to the One who reigns. This is the One who sought us and called us by name. This One rustled in our lives and got our attention, and, in turning to this One, we found life and joy and salvation!

Christian worship is founded on God's revelation of self in Jesus Christ, and involves our corporate response, turning our attention together in praise, as those who have come to know this One as savior, redeemer, and friend. In worship we turn our attention toward the divine other, the holy one in our midst, joining the eternal chorus of praise to the One we have come to know as Father, Son, and Holy Spirit. Worship is, therefore, one of the central ways the Christian church bears witness to the presence of the living God in our world today. In worship we give a name to the "intentional agent in our midst," the creator, redeemer, and sustainer of all things, the One for whom our hearts long.

In worship we show and tell the story of a God who has sought us out; a God who has entered human history in order to rescue, redeem, heal, and save. In worship, we publicize the good news of the reality and availability of the reign of God revealed in the life, death, resurrection, and ascension of Jesus Christ. In worship, we re-present God to the world, making God known through our prayer and praise; through the reading

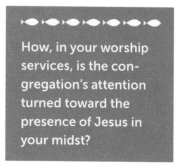

How, in your worship services, is the congregation's attention turned toward the presence of Jesus in your midst?

and preaching of the Word; through the arts, drama, and symbolic action; through the fellowship we share with Christ and one another through the Spirit; through economic sharing, collecting, and distributing of gifts to the poor in imitation of the God who gives good gifts to God's children and cares for the orphan and widow; and through the breaking of bread at the table and drinking from the cup of the Lord. Christian worship is Christian witness. Christian worship is a witness to all the peoples of the earth that the God who seeks our attention is not an unknown *other*, but One who loves us and desires to dwell among us. His name is Immanuel; he is God with us.

The way Luke tells the story in his gospel and in the book of Acts, the ascension of the risen Jesus becomes the source and foundation of Christian worship. In her book *A Royal Waste of Time*, Marva Dawn writes:

> For Luke the ascension is the key... The ascension is so important because that is when Jesus received his glory again... In the ascension Jesus again became the resplendent Lord of the kingdom and made all its joys available to us."[3]

In one of the earliest recorded Christian worship songs, the ascension of Jesus is identified as the energizing source of Christian praise that brings glory to God the Father and bears witness to Jesus's exalted position as the world's true Lord. Our witness of worship is witness to the risen, ascended Jesus, the One who emptied himself, becoming obedient to death; the One who now reigns on high and will one day come back to reign on earth as he now reigns in heaven. Our witness of worship is therefore a witness to the kingdom of God and its present and coming King, Jesus.

The ascension of Jesus is also the starting place of the Christian mission of witness. "Don't just stand there staring up in the sky," the angels say in Acts 1:11. "It's time to go!"

"You will be my witnesses," Jesus had told them, "in Jerusalem, and in all Judea and Samaria, and to the ends of the earth." We are sent into the world as worshipers who come together regularly, most often on the first day of the week, to proclaim the praises of our risen King.

Many of the world's global cities today are crowded with people who have yet to recognize the presence of the risen and ascended Jesus who is right now active in the world through the Spirit to liberate, rescue, redeem, and save. These people's "agency detection devices" are not tuned to the activity and presence of the Holy Spirit.

Vancouver is a city full of people who are spiritual seekers. Vancouver is a city full of gods—literally filled with idols. If you walk into any number of restaurants or grocery stores in East Vancouver you will see an idol to the land Buddha on the floor, or a representation of the sky Buddha near the ceiling. You might see a portrait of Krishna on the wall or a Sikh guru. People are trying to connect spiritually, but they do not know that Jesus is the one seeking them!

Our God desires to be known. God created us to know and be known. Jesus came and walked among us, not as some spiritual ghost that goes bump in the night, but as a real, flesh-and-blood person so we could know what God is like. God is seeking us. As Christians, we believe that true human fulfillment and flourishing will not happen until all the nations come to know and worship the true and living God. God is seeking worshipers.

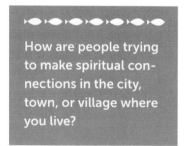

How are people trying to make spiritual connections in the city, town, or village where you live?

In the Old Testament story of the people of Israel, we learn that one of Israel's purposes is to proclaim God's glory among the nations *through their worship*, so that God's glory can fill all space and all history and bring God's joy and peace to the nations.[4] Consider Psalm 96:

Sing to the LORD a new song;

  sing to the LORD, all the earth.

Sing to the LORD, praise his name;

  proclaim his salvation day after day.

Declare his glory among the nations,
his marvelous deeds among all peoples.
For great is the LORD and most worthy of praise;
he is to be feared above all gods.
For all the gods of the nations are idols,
but the LORD made the heavens.
Splendor and majesty are before him;
strength and glory are in his sanctuary.
Ascribe to the LORD, all you families of nations,
ascribe to the LORD glory and strength.
Ascribe to the LORD the glory due his name;
bring an offering and come into his courts.
Worship the LORD in the splendor of his holiness;
tremble before him, all the earth.
Say among the nations, "The LORD reigns."
The world is firmly established, it cannot be moved;
he will judge the peoples with equity.

Mission happens, it is often said, because worship does not. Our worship *is* witness when we show and tell the world the good news about God's reign and invite others to join the praise. The worship of the Christian church is witness to outsiders, forgetters, and the beloved children of the church.

In his book *The Best Kept Secret of Christian Mission*, John Dickson, who is a New Testament scholar and evangelist from Australia, tells the story of his friend Emma, who, in his words, was "a groovy young mum" who worked as a TV producer in his city. When John met Emma, she claimed to be an atheist. In one of their first important conversations, she said to John, "Look, I'm an atheist, I was raised an atheist, so don't bother trying to convert me, will you!"[5]

One Sunday, Emma came to the church John attended in order to support some mutual friends whose child was being baptized. The baptismal ceremony was not the focus of the service; it was included as one of the kinds of things many congregations do week after week: announcements, singing, reading of Scripture, praying, collecting offerings, and preaching.

Emma could count on two fingers the number of church services she had been to over the years, but she left that worship service, in her words, "struck by the spiritual feeling of it all." She came back the next week, and the next, and the next. Each week she said the same thing [to John]: "Look, I'm not religious, but boy, I like this stuff!"[6]

Emma's agency detection device was going off in her brain, alerting her to the deepest longings of her heart. Through the worship service she became attentive to the presence of the Lord who loved her and sought her. She returned to that church for worship over and over again. Emma has since become a follower and worshiper of Jesus Christ. It didn't happen all at once but slowly, over time.

For Emma, it was the very thing she once disdained—a Christian worship service—that drew her into fellowship with the risen, ascended Christ. The worship services Emma attended were not "seeker-friendly" services, specifically designed to reach outsiders. They were simply the normal, weekly services of a local church, where praise and worship, confession and prayer, the preaching of the Word, and fellowship at the table were faithfully practiced. These worship services were led by ordinary, humble women and men of God. But it was precisely in the context of the ordinary witness of worship that Emma became attentive to the God of redeeming love in her midst; to the One for whom her heart longed. The worship of a people who declared the glory of God, and told the story of Jesus, bore witness to this God who sought her, in love. This is our witness of worship.

For outsiders, it may be a weekday ministry of your local church that will make the first connection, long before they enter a Sunday worship service. Many of the outsiders who found their way into worship services in Vancouver have done so through the classes where they come to learn and practice their English.

The Vancouver church regularly has men and women in worship services who have never heard the story of Jesus before but who come because of the relationships that are built through outreach to our immigrant neighbors. In the worship service, they are hearing for the first time the name of the God who loves them and has been seeking them. In worship they begin to understand why these people are so hospitable and kind. Worship that is witness is directed to God, not pitched to outsiders. But it is *for* outsiders, in the sense that, in worship, we invite them to come, taste, and see that the Lord is good.

Visitors to church can easily feel threatened if they suspect the whole event is pitched at them. But when they feel the freedom simply to observe what Christians do—praying to the Lord, giving thanks to him, listening to his Word—visitors are often more at ease, less defensive and more open to the things they hear.[7]

Christian worship is also witness to forgetters, those who once may have been part of the church, may have some knowledge of or experience with God, but who no longer actively participate in the witness of worship. And because they ceased to worship, eventually, they forgot about God.

In the summer of 2006, LifeWay Research conducted a survey of 469 formerly churched adults in North America to better understand what it would take to bring them back. "We were delighted to see such a large percentage of the formerly churched willing to consider church again in the future," said Scott McConnell, who directed the research. The most common motivation of those who would consider returning was "to bring me closer to God."[8]

Cloe was a forgetter who found her way into the worship service in Vancouver through the invitation of an acquaintance who didn't even attend the church. Disgusted by the abuse and corruption of the church she grew up in as a child in Quebec, Cloe stayed away from church for years. But she retained a love for Jesus and a desire to know more about the God she first heard about as a child. Now, as an adult, she was searching for a way to reconnect with God.

During the singing of the hymn "Great Is Thy Faithfulness" in the morning worship service, Cloe's heart was flooded by the presence of the Holy Spirit, and she made the decision to continue worshiping the risen, ascended Christ with our church. On Easter Sunday, that congregation offers adult forgetters the opportunity to remember their baptism during the baptismal service. One Easter, Cloe stood before the congregation and reaffirmed her baptismal vows, publicly confessing her faith in Jesus Christ and her desire to live as a faithful follower of Jesus. Year after year, there are an increasing number of adult forgetters in Vancouver who want to reaffirm the faith of their

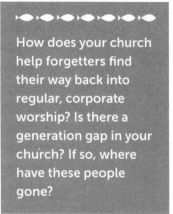

How does your church help forgetters find their way back into regular, corporate worship? Is there a generation gap in your church? If so, where have these people gone?

childhood, a faith that perhaps grew cold for a season but has been rekindled through active participation in the life and worship of the local church.

The regular, faithful—at times, predictable—Sunday worship service is witness to forgetters who find their way into the service through the invitation of a friend or other means. Churches need to be attentive to the forgetters among them. They may have been away for a while, but we want them to know they are welcomed back when they return.

The weekly worship service is also witness to the beloved children of the community, young and old. In worship we witness to one another of all that we have seen, heard, and experienced. In worship our children learn the story of God through singing the songs of our faith. They see the generosity of God in action as we collect offerings and tell stories of how these gifts are used for the life of the world. They listen to the stories of the Bible and how these words apply to our lives through the reading and preaching of the Word. They experience the *holy other* through artistic and symbolic expressions of God's presence. They learn to pray as they overhear the prayers of the people.

Our children are affirmed as full participants in the community of worship through baptism in a worship service, and are encouraged to share their gifts in the worship service as musicians, Scripture readers, ushers, or performers of dramatic arts. Regular and active participation in Sunday worship is one of the primary sources of spiritual formation for our children, youth, and adults.

As a child in the church, I learned about God's grace by singing the hymn "Wonderful Grace of Jesus." I still remember my dad holding the hymnal for me and following his finger as they passed over these words: "Wonderful the matchless grace of Jesus, deeper than the mighty rolling sea! Higher than the mountain, sparkling like a fountain, all sufficient grace for even me (for even me)!"[9]

I recently overheard my elementary-age son singing to himself in the other room: "Jesus, he can move the mountains; Our God is mighty to save, he is mighty to save,"[10] a song that is popular in the church today. The songs change, but the spiritual formation of worship remains. Our worship is witness to our children, youth, and adults, to all the beloved children of the church.

Worship that is witness is worship that shapes the lives of Christians in the world as witnesses after the pattern of our worship. In other words, the worship service itself equips us for our witness in the world. "Gathered in the community of saints, we are formed by the truth taught in worship's music and word to be Church so that out of our Christian character will flow the witness of our words and deeds for the sake of the world," writes Marva Dawn.[11] One of the best ways to equip a congregation for their witness in the world is regular, corporate worship. The rhythm of Christian discipleship moves from worship to witness. We come, week after week, gathered in the presence of the risen Lord, and are sent back into the world to represent God's reign on earth as it is in heaven. Every week we engage in the pattern of discipleship that we see in Jesus's own ministry with his twelve disciples and the seventy-two in Luke 10: gathered to Jesus, sent by Jesus; gathered to Jesus, sent by Jesus. We are gathered in worship then sent as his redemptive agents in the world, as his witnesses.

In many cities in North America, people have by and large ceased to make time for worship. This makes what the church does on Sunday mornings, or at other gathering times during the week, more important than ever before. But it is not easy to maintain a regular worshiping community today. There is so much pressure on families, like mine, to cut worship out of the calendar and fill Sunday mornings with other things. To participate in the witness of worship will cost our congregants something. But we need to help our congregations see that their regular, faithful participation in worship is witness to the God who draws and calls all nations and all peoples, young and old, to himself. Pastors and worship leaders need to continue to renew their worship service so they can witness to the gospel in ways that communicate effectively in their contexts and build up their communities of faith for their common witness.

Paul Chilcote illustrates the formational importance of the church in worship in an article titled "The Integral Nature of Worship and Evangelism." He retells a story told to him, about Frank and Nellie Baker, who served a small Methodist church on the northeast coast of England during World War II. A prisoner-of-war camp was located near their home, and Frank and Nellie felt called by God to reach out to these captured soldiers. So they went to the prison commander and received permission to take a different German prisoner with them to church each Sunday, and then to their home afterward for a meal. So, throughout the whole of World War II, the Bakers ministered to and hosted a number of various German soldiers, one of whom happened to be Jürgen Moltmann. Moltmann went on to become one of the greatest theologians of the twentieth century, writing passionately of a Christian theology of hope in the midst of a world gone wrong. And, according to Moltmann himself, as Chilcote writes the story, "The seed of hope was planted in my heart around Frank and Nellie Baker's Sunday dinner table."[12]

The Bakers lived the integral nature of worship and [witness]. I am absolutely sure that, if you had asked, "What are you doing?" Frank or Nellie would have said, "Well, we are simply doing what Christians do. We are spending time together in the worship of our good God, breaking bread together and eating our food with glad and generous hearts."[13]

Historically, Christian worship has consisted of two movements: Word and Table. The communion table represents the integral nature of worship and witness. Eugene Peterson speaks to this when he writes:

We become present to what God intends to do with and for us through worship, become present to the God who is present to us… We bring ourselves to the eucharistic table and enter into that grand fourfold shape of the liturgy that shapes us: taking, blessing, breaking, and giving—the life of Jesus taken and blessed, broken and [given]. That eucharistic life now shapes our lives as we give ourselves, Christ in us, to be taken, blessed, broken, and [given] in lives of witness and service, justice and healing.[14]

> ▸◆▸◆▸◆▸◆▸◆▸◆▸◆
>
> In what ways has God taken, blessed, broken, and given you for the life of the world? Try sharing your personal story using these four words as an outline to shape the narrative flow of your story.

Taken, blessed, broken, and given. On the night of his resurrection, Jesus appears among his disciples behind locked doors in the room where they shared the Passover meal together three days before. Who is this One who has appeared in their midst? As Jesus speaks, they begin to recognize him. This is the one sent from the Father to reveal God to the world. The Father took, blessed, broke, and gave Jesus, for the life of the world. Jesus now sends us the same way, as witnesses. It is through our corporate worship that we bear witness to the God who takes, blesses, breaks, and gives. It is through worship that we are now taken, blessed, broken, and given, for the life of the world. This is our witness of worship.

3 ❀ Our Witness of Wonder

Acts 2:17: In the last days, God says, I will pour out my Spirit on all people. Your sons and daughters will prophesy, your young men will see visions, your old men will dream dreams.

My friends Benji and Abbi live as witnesses to the good news of the kingdom of God in one of the most spiritually challenging places on the planet. It is not a country where Christians are imprisoned or killed for their faith, nor is it a tribal culture where local shamans ward off evil spirits. In fact, they live in the Capitol Hill neighborhood of Seattle, Washington, in the United States, where, in Benji's words, "intellectualism, the occult, materialism, apathy, addiction, brokenness, deceit and religious woundings have combined to create a canyon between this land and divine Love."[1]

In Benji's neighborhood, and perhaps where you live, most of his neighbors are either turned off by or tuned out to the church, preachers, and Christians in general. Realizing this, instead of opening a church, Benji and Abbi opened a community living room where they serve coffee and hold conversations about whatever is on people's hearts and minds. Their purpose was not to move to Capitol Hill and start doing things to try and reach people but to simply sit there for a while: meeting, loving, listening to, and serving their neighbors. As Benji and Abbi began to live and move among the people of their neighborhood, building friendships rooted in genuine love and mutual respect, they began to discover that many of the people in their neighborhood were in pain of some kind, whether physical, emotional, mental, relational, or spiritual. The pain of his neighbors troubled Benji: "How do I confront intense problems like mental illness, cancer, depression, skepticism, unbelief, and so forth?" he asked himself.[2] He felt powerless. The heavy, gray clouds of Seattle mirrored the spiritually oppressive mists that clouded his own soul.

One day, while Benji prayed for his neighbors, he began to sense the Holy Spirit interceding for *him*, praying for him, and he says that as he prayed, he caught the sound of the conversation going on between Father, Son, and Holy Spirit.[3] Romans 8:26-27 came to his mind, where Paul writes:

In the same way, the Spirit helps us in our weakness. We do not know what we ought to pray for, but the Spirit himself intercedes for us through wordless groans. And he who searches our hearts knows the mind of the Spirit, because the Spirit intercedes for God's people in accordance with the will of God.

As he prayed, Benji felt suddenly affirmed and reminded that he was a son of the King of kings and Lord of lords. He was the child of a King who understood the challenges he faced in Capitol Hill. This same King once moved into a neighborhood in first-century Palestine, lived among a people in pain, poured himself out on their behalf, emptied himself for the life and healing of the world. This King suffered and died for the world he loved. But death could not defeat him! This King ascended to the right hand of God the Father almighty, where he now intercedes on behalf of those he loves. This King gives gifts to his children for their work and witness in the world, the gift of the Holy Spirit.

This realization was a great encouragement to Benji. "To be Christian is to be filled with the power of God and endued with the gifts of the Holy Spirit," he writes in his book, *The Fire Reply*.

[God] has given us his Holy Spirit and an anointing which has furnished us with the powers and gifts necessary to carry on doing what Jesus was doing on the earth…setting captives free, bringing healing, deliverance, truth and liberty. It is humbling to think that we have been made capable of carrying on the ministry of Jesus in the same way that he ministered. But it's very true.[4]

This realization transformed Benji and Abbi's witness where they live. Their ministry now focuses on prayer, interceding for and praying for those in pain, joining their prayers with the prayers of the Father, Son, and Holy Spirit. Their prayer is that God's kingdom would come and God's will be done in their city as it is in heaven. Rather than try to convince people that Jesus is Savior, talking at people whose ears are closed and whose resistance is up to Christians, Benji and Abbi humbly seek to demonstrate Jesus's saving power through simple prayers for people who are in pain. Their mission is to set captives free, releasing those held prisoner by an enemy who blinds them to the truth of the gospel. Benji regularly prays for people in pain, wherever he meets them, whether in a coffee shop or as part of their worship gatherings.

But physical healing is not the main point of Benji and Abbi's ministry. They understand their offer of healing as witness to the wonderful and healing and saving and delivering good news of the reign of God now at work in the world through the Son, by the Spirit. "In the gospels," Benji writes, "healing is simply one of God's obvious manners of revealing his nature, his will, demonstrating his goodness and his kingdom, and meeting people in their pain and cry for relief and 'saving.'"[5]

After several years, they formed a worshiping community on Capitol Hill, offering their church as a community of healing, calling themselves The Church of the Undignified as a sign that their church is for people who don't have it all together; a church for people in pain; a church for people who need the wondrous work of the Spirit in their lives to make them whole. The small and humble Christian community that now gathers in their neighborhood under Benji and Abbi's pastoral care participate in a witness of wonder. In their context, this wonder comes through being attentive to the power and presence of the Spirit at work among them, and forming a community where the healing power of the Spirit is offered to people in physical, emotional, spiritual, relational, or economic pain.

You can't read the book of Acts without noticing that the witness of the early Christian church goes hand in hand with signs and wonders, including physical healing, deliverance from the demonic, restoration of damaged and broken lives, and the spread of new communities throughout the Greco-Roman world that are filled with wonder, love, and praise.

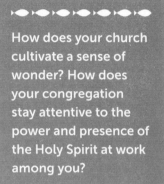

How does your church cultivate a sense of wonder? How does your congregation stay attentive to the power and presence of the Holy Spirit at work among you?

Signs and wonders continue to be a vital part of the witness of the church in many parts of our world today. But as someone who was raised in North America, my education has trained me to be skeptical about claims of the miraculous. There are many religious charlatans in the world today who promise miracles as a way to fatten their wallets, widen their fan bases, and satiate their lust for power. Because of this, many Christians are cautious and suspicious of churches that promote themselves as being places of miracles. In some churches and public ministries, the promise of miraculous healing or material prosperity has been horribly twisted to be seen as a sign of a person's individual level of faith, not as a sign of the in-breaking kingdom of God. So it is right to be cautious and discerning. Yet, I'm becoming more and more convinced that, in a context where—on one hand people believe faith to be irrational, and on the other hand people are coming from cultures attuned to the spirit world—perhaps signs and wonders are needed today to open blind eyes and unstop deaf ears and set captives free. After all, wonder is at the heart of the revelation of God in the world.

Pentecost itself is a wonder-filled event that bears witness to the coming of the promised reign of God in the world. Think about what happens on Pentecost in Acts 2:1-4: *a sound like the blowing of a violent wind*; something that *seemed to be tongues of fire that separated and came to rest on* Jesus's followers; the sudden ability to speak in other languages and bear witness to the story of Jesus's *wonderful* reign!

"What in the world was going on here?" the people of Jerusalem wonder. "Are these people drunk?" they ask. No, it isn't something "in the world" that is going on here! If you know the story, then you know that what is going on at Pentecost is the intersection of two worlds, heaven and earth coming together in the formation of a wonder-filled new community, instituted by Christ and constituted by the Holy Spirit. This community will be characterized by eschatological joy, the joy of the last day when God sets the world right again and brings healing to all the nations of the earth. The joy of the emerging Christian community is a wondrous witness to the people in Jerusalem, Judea, Samaria, and the ends of the earth, who witness in the life of the early Christian community the power and presence of the Holy Spirit.

The way Luke tells the story in Acts, the wonderful events of Pentecost are a consequence of the ascension of the risen Jesus to the throne of heaven. In the Old Testament, the ascension of a new king to the throne is followed by the distribution of gifts to the people, celebrating the consolidation of the king's reign. Pentecost fulfills the wondrous promise given to Israel that God will return and take his rightful place as the long-awaited and promised King. And when the King takes his throne, he gives gifts to the people.

The gift that the people of Israel have been looking forward to is the gift of the Holy Spirit. In Ezekiel 36:26, the LORD promises: "I will give you a new heart and put a new spirit in you; I will remove from you your heart of stone and give you a heart of flesh." The Spirit will enable the people of Israel to live under the peaceable rule and reign of God, cleansed from sin, filled with the life and love of God, able to keep the LORD's command to live together as lights that shine brightly in the midst of the darkened world. The Spirit will make them a holy people unto the LORD, a people among whom God will live, by the Spirit. Arriving at the end of his journey, Jesus pours out the Holy Spirit upon the disciples, and the Christian church is born. This is a community created to show and tell the wondrous presence of the kingdom of God on earth, and to announce and demonstrate the coming reign of Christ to all the nations of the earth. They are to live together as witnesses of wonder.

In the Old Testament, the temple is a place of wonder where the Majestic Glory dwells. Like ancient Israel and the early church, we were created to be a community that is attentive to God's wondrous presence among us, and to witness to God's presence in the lives of those whom God is drawing into the triune life. Our God is wondrously at work in the world around us and in the lives of our friends, neighbors, coworkers, and family. When the Spirit of God is preveniently working in the lives of our children, friends, neighbors, coworkers, classmates, and acquaintances, it is our calling, as a community of wonder, to be attentive to this work of the Spirit and act as midwives, of sorts, helping to bring the new life of the Spirit to birth.

> How would you describe your experience of the Holy Spirit? Where or when do you feel most spiritually alive?

My friend Ming is a follower of Jesus today through the midwifery of his Christian friend Peter and a church in Walla Walla that was attentive to the wondrous work of the Spirit in Ming's life. Ming grew up in Hong Kong. Life was very hard for Ming and his family. He worked to help support the family when he was only six years old. When Ming was eleven, he began hanging around with a gang. He was later charged with possession of an illegal weapon and given ten strokes with a cane by the police. Ming says at that time, he began to realize he needed to change his life. He could see that his life was headed nowhere.

When Ming was seventeen years old, his family was approved to come to the United States. Ming hoped that coming to the U.S. would enable him to change his life and get a new start. But once in the States, he was recruited by a Chinese "association" in Seattle's Chinatown that hired new immigrants to do their dirty work, including illegal gambling, smuggling, or worse. T h i n g s went from bad to worse for Ming in the States; it was not the place of salvation and opportunity he had hoped it would be, and his life remained dark and hopeless.

One night, with his life unraveling, Ming says he remembers standing on his back porch, staring into the night sky and calling out to the sky god of his religious upbringing for help. He told the sky god that he hated his life and wanted to change. He had done this many times before in the Buddhist temples in Hong Kong, but this time he was not facing the Buddha statues; he stood on his back porch and cried out into the dark, starry night sky. One week after this prayer, while wandering around the streets of Chinatown, Ming ran into the wife of the one friend he had in the whole United States who was a Christian—a man named Peter.

Peter lived in Walla Walla, and his wife, Millie, happened to be visiting Seattle that day. Was it coincidence that they just happened to see each other on the street that day, or was it the wondrous work of the Spirit on Ming's behalf to heal, liberate, redeem, and save? Ming desperately wanted to get out of Seattle, so he asked Millie if he could come visit them in Walla Walla. She agreed, so after borrowing thirty dollars from his mother, Ming took the bus to eastern Washington. When Ming's friend Peter saw him, he could see that Ming was not doing well, and he gave Ming a job washing dishes in his restaurant.

Looking for help to get his life together, Ming took his friend's advice and found a local church. It happened to be a Nazarene church. For the next year, Ming went to church each week and, through their witness of worship, began to hear stories about Jesus Christ and the power of the Holy Spirit to heal, transform, and change lives. During this time, Ming had many bad dreams about the things he had done in his life. When he told a Christian friend about his nightmares, his friend was attentive to the work of the Spirit in Ming's life. He suggested that in response to these nightmares, Ming should talk to Jesus, ask forgiveness for the things he had done, be baptized, and receive the Holy Spirit.

Ming went to the pastor and said, "I want to be baptized." The pastor took time to share the story of Jesus with Ming and asked Ming if he would like to receive Jesus as Savior and Lord. Ming became a follower of Jesus in May of 1991, and was baptized soon after. By the time I met him a decade later, Ming was well established in his faith and hungry to grow in his walk with Jesus.

Prayers in the night. Coincidental encounters. Dreams. A desire to be changed from the inside out. The Spirit was wondrously at work in Ming's life. Thankfully, Ming's Christian friends Millie and Peter and the Nazarene church in Walla Walla were attentive to the wondrous work of the Spirit in Ming's life and were able to share the hope of Jesus Christ and the promised gift of the Spirit with him. Ming's story always reminds me to be attentive to the wondrous work of the Spirit in the lives of the people around me.

We live in a wondrous world. Thomas Long reminds us that:

> In terms of contemporary religious experience, the world is full of... events in nature, personal experience, and history that point toward the mystery of God... A daffodil opens in all its spring beauty and glory, a troubled relationship is healed, a child is born—all these experiences and countless others

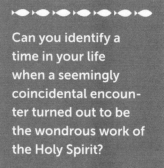

Can you identify a time in your life when a seemingly coincidental encounter turned out to be the wondrous work of the Holy Spirit?

draw our attention to the divine mystery that pervades and pushes through human events.[6]

But without the witness of a Spirit-filled community, people would not recognize these wondrous moments for what they are. Our witness of wonder must include Spirit-empowered words of wonder, when we humbly yet confidently call attention to the life and work of the Spirit of God in the world around us.

In 1 Peter 3:15, Peter writes: "Always be prepared to give an answer to everyone who asks you to give the reason for the hope that you have. But do this with gentleness and respect." We bear witness to the wondrous work of the Spirit with our lips. Through words of wonder, we share a wondrous hope that includes:

- the coming kingdom of God that is turning the world right side up again;
- eternal life given as a gift of God's Spirit as we are drawn into the loving fellowship of Father, Son, and Holy Spirit, from whom not even death can separate us;
- forgiveness of sin that makes us right with God and the ongoing transformation of life from the inside out, renewing us into the wondrous image and likeness of Christ;
- healing for those in pain, restoration of broken relationships, and the making of all things new;
- finding meaning and purpose in life through active participation in the life and mission of God for the life of the world;
- a community empowered to live the joy-filled life of the Spirit in mutual love and common service to one another.

Our witness is not always filled with wonder, though. We need to grapple with the fact that the way we often imagined witnessing in the church is by using words aimed at the head, based on rational argument and salesmanship-like persuasion, using logic to convince people to give their assent to a set of facts—rather than opening a window to the wondrous work of God in the world, through the Son, by the Spirit.

In my experience I'm not finding that logic-based, rational approach to witnessing is very helpful today. Pressure techniques, salesmanship, and rationale are not cutting it. These methods turn people off and push them away. But people *are* hungry for a connection with the divine. They are open to spiritual conversations if you take time to build trust and show genuine interest in people as individuals, not simply as objects to be reached.

The cities in the Pacific Northwest have a relatively low percentage of Christians but a high percentage of people who seek authentic spirituality. People do have questions about the spiritual life and how to overcome the barriers in their lives that hinder their fulfillment and joy. People do wonder about life and death and whether there is a power greater than them at work in the world. But people want to be listened to, not just talked to. They are in pain and looking for healing. Who will listen? Who will pray? Who will heal? These are the things a church that lives in the wonder of the Spirit has to offer! The Christian church is not offering an invitation to join a religious club, or even to help people punch a ticket to heaven. We offer an encounter with the risen and ascended Christ, who transforms us, and who will one day transform the whole creation. The King who reigns is coming with healing in his wings! We are agents of the One who gives generously of the Holy Spirit to all who ask, seek, and knock.

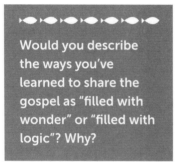

Would you describe the ways you've learned to share the gospel as "filled with wonder" or "filled with logic"? Why?

Our witness of wonder must include words of wonder that speak of this coming King and the life of the Spirit. In 2 Corinthians 4:2, Paul reminds the Corinthians that he does not use cunning speech when he shares the gospel, nor does he distort the word of God, but sets forth the truth plainly. Paul understands that if the veil of unbelief is going to be lifted from the eyes of unbelievers, it will come as a wondrous gift of God, whose light shines in the darkness. Paul speaks with simple faith and a humble confidence that God is wonderfully at work in the world, and "that the grace that is reaching more and more people may cause thanksgiving to overflow to the glory of God" (2 Corinthians 4:15).

Perhaps we need to be encouraged and trained and equipped in how to share Jesus out of our own sense of wonder, the wonder of our own shared participation in the life and love of God, infused with the wondrous stories of Jesus in the Bible, with confidence that God's grace is being poured out all around us. We prepare ourselves to give an account of the wondrous hope we have in Jesus Christ by familiarizing ourselves with the broad outline of the gospel as summarized in the apostolic preaching in Acts and in the Gospels themselves. These passages tell the wondrous story of Jesus, who lived, died, rose from the grave, and is coming again to renew the whole creation. Building on these stories, we then share the wondrous story of how Jesus has renewed and transformed our lives and communities. Our witness of wonder is, therefore, intimately connected to our own spiritual formation.

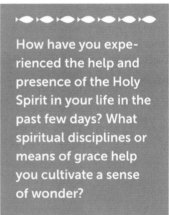

How have you experienced the help and presence of the Holy Spirit in your life in the past few days? What spiritual disciplines or means of grace help you cultivate a sense of wonder?

In the New Testament, signs and wonders of the kingdom and words of wonder are always accompanied by, infused with, and surrounded by prayer. Prayer is, therefore, an essential part of the witness of wonder of the Christian church. One of the early fathers of the church, Clement of Alexandria, once said that "prayer is keeping company with God."[7] This insight helped former Regent College president James Houston understand prayer as a transforming friendship with God. "Christian prayer is prayer to the Father, through the Son, by the Holy Spirit," writes Houston.[8] It is prayer to the Father, through the Son, by the Holy Spirit that shapes us to be a people who bear witness to the wondrous presence of God in the world. A community that prays is a witness to the wondrous presence of God.

The beloved children of the church need our witness of wonder. Children are natural wonderers. They come into this world full of wonder and open to the reality of a God who seeks to share life with them. We need to nurture this sense of wonder in our children and youth through our life together in our homes and churches. Teaching our children and youth to pray and to be attentive to the voice and presence of the Spirit is a way to nurture them in the witness of wonder.

Christian adults need to retain the wonder of childlike faith. In adult spiritual formation groups and Bible studies, take time to witness to one another the wondrous presence of God at work among you. When you gather in small groups or Sunday school classes, encourage and be encouraged to share where and how you have sensed the work of the Spirit in your lives since the last meeting. As you share your stories of how the Spirit is at work in your life and how you are attentive to the Spirit in the wider world, you are engaging in a witness of wonder to one another.

When adults lose their sense of wonder, they easily become forgetters. Forgetters need to be reminded of the wonder that perhaps once touched their lives but no longer characterizes their relationship with God. In Revelation 3:20, Jesus is pictured knocking at the door of a house that has shut him out. This was written to the church in Laodicea, a church that has grown lukewarm because of its comfort and prosperity. It is a church in danger of forgetting the wonder of their first love. Forgetters need to be reminded of the promise, wonder, and hope of the Spirit-filled life. Sometimes, like in the book of Revelation, this includes warnings and signs and wonders that are intended to get the attention of those who slumber in their faith. The fear of the LORD is part of our witness of wonder, in particular among forgetters who at one time held the LORD in reverence.

Miracles, prayer, and words of wonder also witness to outsiders whom God seeks to include and enfold into God's divine life. Our witness of wonder includes the wondrous good news that those who were once outsiders to the covenant people of God are now included. Through the new birth of the Spirit of God, outsiders become insiders in God's kingdom.

Wouldn't it be wonderful to find, in our divided, fractured, and religiously violent world, a community in which everyone— the beloved children of the church, forgetters, and outsiders—was welcomed, loved, and included? A community that was inclusive of all, no matter how old or young, not divided by social status or income level? A community where Africans, North and South Americans, Europeans, Asians, Islanders, Israelis, Arabs, and First Nations persons lifted their voices together in wonder, love, and praise? Would not such a community be full of wonder? Is not the breaking down of ethnic barriers, the honoring of the aged, the empowerment of the youth, the embracing of the poor, the communion of people of differing abilities, incomes, and political viewpoints, wonderful (as in, *full of wonder*)? A community of inclusion and Trinitarian hospitality, where there is a place at the table for everyone? Is this not what God seeks to do in the world today? Forming new communities in all the cities, suburban, and rural towns of our world as embassies of God's wondrous, inclusive life and love?

This is a wonder-filled vision of the church. The wonder to which we bear witness flows from the church being an inclusive, Spirit-filled community, who live their lives together, in this world, as witness to the wondrous reign of God in Christ, by the Spirit. This is our witness of wonder.

 ## 4 ° Our Witness of Way

---

*Acts 2:44-45: All the believers were together and had
everything in common. They sold property and possessions
to give to anyone who had need.*

As a young boy, Jesse was offered music therapy by the Variety
Club, housed in the Academy of Music, a prestigious institute in
Vancouver. The Variety Club had contributed a substantial sum
of money toward the purchase and construction of the facility
with the agreement that the academy would provide space for
music therapy for at least ten years for students who, like Jesse,
have a mental handicap. A short while after taking Jesse to attend
classes, his mother was asked to bring him in by the back door and
wait in the hallway, instead of coming through the main door and
waiting in the reception area. Apparently, Jesse's presence made
other patrons uncomfortable. His mother refused.

Over the years, attitudes toward people with mental disabili-
ties have changed. Jesse's mother has experienced more tolerance
and sometimes acceptance but never excitement over Jesse's presence. She has frequently been thanked for removing Jesse when
requested because he is too small, too big, too young, too old, too
low functioning, too uncooperative. When Jesse requested to attend the church his autistic friend Geoffrey attended, his mother,

who did not attend church, was reluctant and apprehensive but felt she had an obligation to honor the request.

From his first Sunday, the congregation welcomed Jesse with warmth, love, and encouragement. His mother later said to me, "I never expected Jesse to be welcomed with so much respect and worth; to be embraced and encouraged to become part of the church family. This is something that you may see as the way you are, your church's way, but make no mistake: This is not the way of the larger world out there. I have never been thanked for bringing Jesse, nor been told that he has enriched a community, as you and others in your church have said to me." Because of the way the church welcomed Jesse, his mother now attends worship services even when Jesse is unable to. As she explained to me, "I don't know why I want to keep coming here. But there is something going on in your church and worship services, something about the way your congregation lives out your faith, that has become meaningful to me."

Has anyone ever expressed appreciation to you for the way your church lives its life together in the world? If so, what did they appreciate or notice that was different?

Before they are called Christians, the earliest Christian communities instituted by Christ and constituted by the Spirit that spread from Jerusalem through Judea and Samaria to the ends of the earth after Pentecost, are simply known as "those who belong to the Way." Luke summarizes their way of living in Acts 2:42-47:

They devoted themselves to the apostles' teaching and to the fellowship, to the breaking of bread and to prayer. Everyone was filled with awe at the many wonders and signs performed by the apostles. All the believers were together and had everything in common. They sold property and possessions to give to anyone who had need. Every day they continued to meet together in the temple courts. They broke bread in their homes and ate together with glad and sincere hearts, praising God and enjoying the favor of all the people. And the Lord added to their number daily those who were being saved.

Their way of living includes their witness of worship and their witness of wonder, but it also includes fellowship, mutual service, and economic sharing: the distribution of material goods to anyone who has need.

This emerging Jesus community is filled with people who are generous and joyful, whose fellowship is characterized by gladness and sincerity. Their public way of living life together earns these first followers of Jesus goodwill in their city. And the result of the witness of their way of living publicly before a watching world is that *the Lord adds to their number daily those who are being saved.*

Jesus himself set the pattern for their way of living. The way of life of the early church flows from their devotion to the risen and ascended Jesus and their loving obedience to his recent teachings. Each week they gather to worship their ascended Lord. And, through the telling and retelling of the way of Jesus in their public worship and in their homes in private gatherings, they continually rehearse God's generous story and encourage one another to live out the teachings of Jesus in their everyday lives in the world: the way of forgiveness, mercy, reconciliation, and love of enemy. God demonstrated God's way of being in the world through God's Son, Jesus Christ, and now invites the Christian community into this way of being in the world through the power and presence of the Holy Spirit. This, then, is a way of living that flows from the wondrous hope of the gospel: the good news that the kingdom of God has come near in Jesus Christ; that, by the power of the Holy Spirit, God's new creation is breaking into the old; and that we can now, in this life, by the power of the Spirit, begin to live out the life of the kingdom that is coming.

These first followers of Jesus understand that the Christian church is to bring the firstfruits of the coming kingdom of God to fruition in their homes, villages, towns, and cities. They are to be a sign, a pointer, a demonstration garden in the midst of the world, however small and humble and seemingly imperfect. They are mustard seeds, a bit of yeast, seemingly insignificant, but bursting with kingdom potential.

Christopher Wright says:

[Christians] are a representative people. Our task is to represent the living God to the world, and to bring the world to acknowledge the living God... An essential part of the mission of God's people is nothing other than to be what they are—by living out the holiness of God in practical everyday living.[1]

In his book *Evangelism after Christendom*, Bryan Stone writes:

...the most evangelistic thing the church can do today is to be the church—to be formed imaginatively by the Holy Spirit through core practices such as worship, forgiveness, hospitality, and economic sharing into a distinctive people in the world, a new social option, the body of Christ. It is the very shape and character of the church as the Spirit's "new creation" that is the witness to God's reign in the world and so both the source and aim of Christian evangelism.[2]

In other words, our ecclesiology (who we are, as the church) is connected to our missiology (what we do, as the church). We do what we are, and we are what we do.

The way of the early church changes the trajectory of the world. "There can be no doubt that it was the changed lifestyle of the early Christians which made such a deep impact upon classical antiquity," writes Michael Green in his book *Evangelism in the Early Church*.[3]

Rodney Stark describes the Greco-Roman world into which the church is born as a place of "squalor, misery, illness, and anonymity."[4] In the pagan world of that day, mercy is regarded as a character defect because mercy is seen as providing unearned help to those in need.[5] In contrast, the earliest Christians teach that God is merciful and that therefore God's people must be merciful. The first church committee ever formed is begun in order to ensure that widows in the community are fed and properly provided for. But it isn't just that the Christians care for and love *one another*. Their care and love extend outside the Christian community.

John Dickson argues that it is the good works of the Christian community that conquer the Roman empire. All around the Mediterranean, churches are setting up food programs, hospitals, and orphanages that are available to believers and unbelievers alike. This is an innovation. Historians often point to ancient Israel as the first society to introduce a comprehensive welfare system that cares for the poor and marginalized within the community. Christians inherit this tradition but open it up to Jew and Gentile, believer and unbeliever alike.[6] The result of this radical care and compassion is that, within two and a half centuries, "Christians had gone from being a small band of several hundred Palestinian Jews to the greatest social force in world history."[7]

But not all the attention their way of life attracted was good. In fact, in the fourth century, the Roman emperor Julian became fearful that Christianity "might take over the world forever by the stealth of good works."[8] The empire was threatened by the growing influence of the church, which led to persecution. But it was the way that Christians faced trials, hardship, and persecution that also contributed to the growth and spread of the early church. As Michael Green writes:

…the capacity of Christians to face criticism, hatred, persecution and death, not just with equanimity but with joy must have had a tremendous impact. We know it did. You could mow these Christians down, you could throw them to the lions, but you could not make them deny their Lord or hate their persecutors… A resolute courage which can endure "as seeing him who is invisible," confident of life after death, has an uncanny effect. It disarms the violence of the tormentors.[9]

This is, of course, the way of the cross. When Christians live the way of the cross—turning the other cheek, going the extra mile, praying for those who persecute them, returning blessings for curses—they bear witness to the reality and possibility of the peaceable rule and reign of God in Christ come near. The way of the cross is the Jesus way. Our witness of way is witness to the way of Jesus.

> If a newcomer attended your church for a month, would they characterize your congregation as peaceable? Why or why not?

It was the Jesus way that inspired Phineas Bresee to start a new church in Los Angeles, California, more than a hundred years ago. In the late 1800s, Bresee was assigned to pastor the Fort Street Methodist Church in Los Angeles, "the best appointment in the conference."[10] From this privileged position, Bresee noticed that Los Angeles was undergoing an urban transformation. New immigrants from Japan and China lived and worked among Hispanics, African Americans, and whites. Along with urbanization came "a growing underclass of urban poor, trapped in cycles of despair, alcohol, and addiction."[11] As a follower of Jesus, Bresee was compelled to respond to the need. But, as a follower of Jesus, he also understood that he could not just swoop in from the outside, remain aloof from the poverty of the city, and magically save souls. That would not be the Jesus way. That would not be the way of the cross. The Jesus way was for the church to become incarnational, to take up residence in the midst of brokenness, eating and drinking and sharing life with outcasts and sinners, demonstrating to new friends a way of living together that was shaped by their vision of the kingdom of God, and inviting them into that way. This is a way of living that is *for* the life of the world. So Bresee resigned his comfortable appointment and started a church in one of the worst parts of the city, calling it the Church of the Nazarene.

"Let the poor be fed and clothed," Bresee wrote, "let us pour out our substances for this purpose; but let us keep heaven open, that they may receive the unspeakable gift of His love, in the transforming power of the Holy Ghost."[12]

The cities and villages the church finds itself in today are places in need of people whose lives together bear witness to the way of Jesus in the world, a people who live in the power of the Holy Spirit, demonstrating to the world through their shared life together what the life of the kingdom of God looks like.

Tragically, I haven't met many very people lately who perceive the Christian church as a people who live the ways of Jesus in the world. In fact, one of the first things I noticed when I moved to Vancouver was how much disdain and distrust of the Christian church existed among my Canadian friends and neighbors. I had neighbors who, knowing I was a pastor, looked at me with suspicion every time I came around. Many of my Canadian friends and neighbors view Christians as narrow-minded, bigoted, myopic, colonial, selfish, and judgmental. But these are not traits we see in Jesus, are they? These are not the fruits of the Spirit. How did the church come to be viewed this way?

Some of it is based on the church's failures to live the Jesus way. In Canada, clergy abuse scandals and the residential school experience of the First Nations people in Canada has soured many people to the church as a whole. Then, there are those who have had personally negative experiences with the church. As a pastor, I've listened to stories of people who have been harmed by division in the church, gossiping, abuse, power grabs, and other political posturing that drove them away. I don't think all of the scorn that is heaped on the church today is warranted, but we need to be humble enough to admit the times when our life together has not witnessed to the ways of the kingdom of God but instead conforms to the corrupt and violent ways of this world. "A divided, split and fighting church has nothing to say or to give to a divided, broken and violent world," suggests Christopher Wright.[13] And where we fall short, we need to confess our faults humbly and seek the promised renewal and correction of the Spirit. A reactionary, defensive church that is unwilling to admit its shortcomings and unwilling to change its ways is not a witness to the way

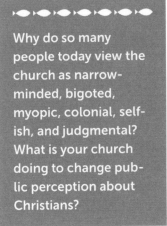

Why do so many people today view the church as narrow-minded, bigoted, myopic, colonial, selfish, and judgmental? What is your church doing to change public perception about Christians?

of the kingdom. The kingdom way includes praying the prayer Jesus taught his disciples, being willing to say to the watching world: "Forgive us our sins, as we forgive those who sin against us."

You see, how we live our lives together, as the church, matters. How we live our lives before a watching world matters. And the way we respond to the changing context, where many are suspicious and hostile toward the church—that matters too. Think for a moment about how a congregation's way of living is witness to the three constituents of the church's witness: the beloved children of the church, forgetters, and outsiders.

The beloved children of our community watch how we live together. Our children and youth pick up cues from our life together as a church community about what being a follower of Jesus looks like and whether they want to be part of a community like this. The Jesus way of living that is witness to the beloved children of the church includes obedience of all the great one-another passages commanded in the New Testament, including:

Mark 9:50—*Be at peace with one another;*

Romans 12:10—*Be devoted to one another* and *honor one another;*

Romans 14:13—*Let us stop passing judgment on one another;*

Romans 15:7—*Accept one another;*

Romans 15:14—*Instruct one another;*

Galatians 5:13—*Serve one another;*

Galatians 5:26—*Do not provoke or envy one another;*

Galatians 6:2—*Carry one another's burdens;*

Ephesians 4:32—*Be kind and compassionate to one other* and *forgive one another;*

Ephesians 5:21—*Submit to one another;*

Colossians 3:9—*Do not lie to one another;*
1 Thessalonians 4:18—*Encourage one another;*
James 4:11—*Do not slander one another;*
James 5:9—*Don't grumble against one another;*
James 5:16—*Pray for one another* and *confess to one another;*
1 Peter 4:9—*Offer hospitality to one another;*

Jesus's command to his disciples in John 13:34 sums up all of these: "A new command I give you: Love one another. As I have loved you, so you must love one another." Jesus himself speaks of the public witness of the way of love when he says in the very next verse, 35: "By this everyone will know that you are my disciples, if you love one another." The way of love is our first witness to the beloved children of the church.

Our love is also witness to forgetters, a witness to those who have walked away from the church. When the Spirit draws lost sons and daughters home, will they find a church that embodies the loving welcome of the Father as in the story of the prodigal son, or will they find the judgmental elder brother?

Kassy was a forgetter whom the Spirit drew home through the witness of our church several years ago. Kassy grew up in a Christian home and was active in the church until, as a young adult, she drifted from God, married a man who was negative about Christianity with whom she had a son, and ended up living in our neighborhood. My wife, Aisling, met Kassy through the local community center soon after we moved to Vancouver, and we frequently ran into her family at community events. Our friendship blossomed on the t-ball field at the local baseball park, where our son Graiden played on the same team with her son, Wyatt. Through conversations at the ballpark, Kassy learned that we pastored a Nazarene church near where she lived.

In 2007, Kassy's marriage broke up, and she found herself in a desperate situation. As she sat at her kitchen table, she remembered the God of her earlier years and found herself saying, "Okay, God, it's time. I'll come back. I'll get to know you again. I'll stop trying to not think about you. I'll stop thinking I don't need you." Because of her friendship with my wife, Kassy knew on that day that it would be the Nazarene church where she would go to find God. On September 9, 2007, Kassy walked through the front doors of our church and found a warm welcome. I still remember the tears when our eyes met in the foyer. She started attending worship services, signed up for a Bible study class, volunteered with children's church, and even found herself on the stage that first year for the Christmas play.

Reflecting on that time, Kassy said to me, "Every moment I was building relationships with women and men of faith who to this day encourage me and help me learn to hear God and believe in his plans for me. I'm so thankful for each one of you." In April of 2008, Kassy watched another woman in our church being baptized. "I remember thinking how cool it was she had decided to do that," she says. This baptism was a witness to Kassy, and she was baptized the very next week!

Kassy kept attending and growing and learning and loving and being loved and noticed how her son, Wyatt, thrived. All the questions he had for her as a toddler about the meaning of life became so much easier for her to answer. As she reengaged the Christian life as an adult, Kassy sought opportunities to learn more about the Jesus way of living through the power of the Spirit. "I decided to take the Alpha course in an effort to gain insight into Christian life from my adult perspective," Kassy remembers. During the Alpha course, Kassy experienced the wondrous, healing power of the Holy Spirit. "The healing night was special. Three ladies in the church—Regina, Sandra, and Jessie—laid hands on me as I prayed for my broken heart to stop giving me physical pain. When I felt the heat come over my chest I wrote it off as embarrassment, but when I woke up the next morning there was no more pain." Kassy wrote that she stuck around our church because we never judged her or turned her away; instead, we invited her and her son into our homes and into our lives.

It was the congregation's way of living that witnessed to a forgetter named Kassy and her son, Wyatt. The love for Kassy and Wyatt expressed through the people of the church opened the way for her to come home to her heavenly Father. This is our witness of way. Forgetters need this witness of way.

This way is a witness to outsiders as well. Outsiders who come into contact with the church wonder if this community is any different from the other communities in which they live and move and have come from. Outsiders live in a broken and divided world. Outsiders live in a world where the powerful dominate the powerless, where people spend massive amounts of time and money amusing themselves, and where loneliness and isolation is a common experience. They tend to wonder, *Is there another way to live?*

Christians who love one another and love their neighbors; who extend themselves beyond their holy huddle; who work for justice and serve with compassion; who eat and drink with sinners; who pour themselves out for the life of the world; who love mercy, do justice, and walk humbly with God—these Christians live as witness to Jesus.

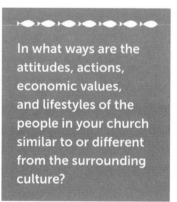

In what ways are the attitudes, actions, economic values, and lifestyles of the people in your church similar to or different from the surrounding culture?

I visited Kenya in November of 2011. In Nairobi I saw a witness of the way of local churches in the slums of Kabete and Kawangware, where congregations have sacrificially started schools to serve children at risk in the community. I saw a witness of the way of the church in Entoronto, where Nazarene Compassionate Ministries is turning a dry and arid land into a green land so families there can learn farming and agriculture. I later returned to Nairobi as part of a team whose assignment was to build a classroom at the Kawangware Church of the Nazarene so they could expand their school. Friends of ours in Vancouver who are not Christians and do not attend our church heard about our project in Kenya and wanted to be part of it, and many of them donated to the cause. Our involvement in this project was a witness to our unchurched neighbors in Vancouver. Our good works are witness to outsiders. Our good works bring glory to God among unbelievers.

In 1 Peter 2:12, Peter encourages Christians to "live such good lives among the pagans that, though they accuse you of doing wrong, they may see your good deeds and glorify God on the day he visits us." Churches all around the world humbly seek to live their common life together in a way that is witness to the beloved children of the church, forgetters, and outsiders. This is our witness of way!

5 ° Evangelism: The Heart of Our Witness

Acts 2:36: Therefore let all Israel be assured of this: God has made this Jesus, whom you crucified, both Lord and Christ.

What comes to mind when you hear the word *evangelism*? Do you have a positive reaction? Negative? Indifferent? Is it is a hopeful and helpful word for you, or a word that raises fear and anxiety? When I asked a group of people in my congregation what the word *evangelism* brought to their minds, I received responses like these:

- Evangelism looks like preaching, Billy Graham, tents and arenas, masses of people.
- Evangelism is someone standing on a street corner handing out tracts.
- Evangelism is intrusive.
- Evangelism is meeting people one on one or buttonholing people in the mall.
- Evangelism is trying to rescue people, like the claw machine at the arcade.

Finally, someone admitted that, "Growing up, I felt a very strong sense of obligation to personally evangelize from the time I was very young. As a result, evangelism has been fairly fraught with anxiety."

As I interviewed people in the church, I began to realize that the word *evangelism* carries some baggage. Someone recently came to me and said, "When I first heard that you were going to preach a series on witness and evangelism, my first reaction was *Oh no, he's going to ask us to go door to door, knocking on the doors of strangers to tell them about Jesus.*" She was relieved I hadn't asked her to do this—and she loves Jesus!

The negativity surrounding the word *evangelism* is even greater outside the church. A good friend of mine in my neighborhood asked me what my doctoral research was about. I said "evangelism" just to see what kind of reaction I would get. I did get a reaction. It wasn't positive. It is sad that evangelism has become a dirty word, a word that provokes anxiety and embarrassment in the church, and is an affront to the world. This realization inspired my research into the problem and my desire to regenerate evangelism as a missional practice of our church. I want to reclaim evangelism as a hope-filled and meaningful practice of the church.

In the Bible, to *evangelize* means literally to announce good news or a welcome message. This is the word often translated as *gospel* in our English Bibles. In the New Testament, the gospel is the good news about the victory of Jesus Christ over the powers of evil, sin, and death; and the saving implications of his life, death, resurrection, ascension, and coming return for the whole world. In Peter's sermon on Pentecost, this good news is centered on the exaltation of Jesus Christ to the right hand of God and the gracious outpouring of the Holy Spirit on all who recognize Jesus as both Lord and Christ. The good news that Peter announces is that Jesus is Israel's long-awaited Messiah and the world's true Lord, the one who brings God's salvation for all who will turn and receive.

The New Testament use of the word *evangelize* is actually rooted in its Old Testament use. Isaiah 52:7 celebrates the bringer of such good news:

How beautiful on the mountains

    are the feet of those who bring good news,

who proclaim peace,
> who bring good tidings,
> who proclaim salvation,
who say to Zion,
> "Your God reigns!"

May 8, 1945, known as V-E Day, was the day celebrated worldwide in honor of Nazi Germany surrendering to the Allies. When news of Germany's surrender was announced, the relief and celebrations occurred throughout the Western world. In the United Kingdom, King George VI and Queen Elizabeth made public appearances on the balcony of Buckingham Palace, along with Prime Minister Churchill. In the United States, it was President Truman's birthday, and he claimed that it was the best birthday he'd ever had.[1] The news of the Allied victory, the news of the enemy's defeat, and the coming peace was *good news.*

Evangelism is rooted in the announcement of the good news that the cosmic victory won by Jesus at the cross has been confirmed through the resurrection of Jesus Christ from the dead. The resurrection and ascension of Jesus, and the consequent outpouring of the Holy Spirit, assure us that the reign of God has begun in Christ Jesus and the reign of evil, sin, and death is ending. This is good news for a world held in the grip of evil, sin, abuse, corruption, and death.

In his book *The Evangelistic Love of God & Neighbor,* Scott Jones helpfully reminds us that this good news is news that reveals and confirms the love of God for the whole human race and the whole creation.

> Why does God announce the coming of [God's] reign in the person of Jesus? Why does Christ die for the redemption of the world? Why does God guarantee the fulfillment of all these promises in a new heaven and new earth? The answer to all these and other fundamental questions lies in God's essence, which is love. God creates, redeems, and saves the world because God is love. God loves the world.[2]

The most well-known expression of this love is found in John 3:16, which beautifully encapsulates this loving good news: "For God so loved the world that he gave his one and only Son, that whoever believes in him shall not perish but have eternal life."

In order to regenerate evangelism as a meaningful practice of our church, we need to rediscover and embrace the gospel for what it truly is: the good news of God's redeeming, reconciling, and rescuing love for the whole creation. The Christian church is called, empowered, and gifted to bear witness to the loving reign of God in many and multiform ways. We bear witness to the reign of God in Christ through our witness of worship, our witness of wonder, and our witness of way.

We often use the word *evangelism* to refer to this wider mission of announcing and embodying this good news in the world. But in order to regenerate evangelism as a missional practice of the church, I want to suggest we use the word *evangelism* to refer to a more focussed mission that stands at the heart of our mission of witness that we engage in as a whole congregation. This more focused mission of evangelism is located scripturally in Matthew 28:18-20, where the risen Jesus says to his disciples:

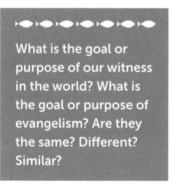

What is the goal or purpose of our witness in the world? What is the goal or purpose of evangelism? Are they the same? Different? Similar?

All authority in heaven and on earth has been given to me. Therefore go and make disciples of all nations, baptizing them in the name of the Father and of the Son and of the Holy Spirit, and teaching them to obey everything I have commanded you. And surely I will be with you always, to the very end of the age.

This passage is often referred to as the Great Commission. As we—a community of disciples—are going together, bearing witness to the reality of the reign of God in the world through our worship, wonder, and way, we are commissioned by the authority of King Jesus to make disciples, inviting others to enter the wondrous life of the kingdom of God, to join us in worship of our risen King, and participate with us on the way with Jesus. If we think about our mission this way, we come to see that evangelism stands at the front end of the disciple-making mission of the church. Evangelism encompasses the work of the whole church in initiating the beloved children of the church, forgetters, and outsiders into Christian discipleship in response to the reign of God in Christ. Our larger mission of witness is therefore intimately connected to our more focussed mission of evangelism. Through our worship, wonder, and way we announce and embody the very same good news of God's reign in Christ that we seek to initiate persons into through our practices of evangelism.

I am not actually suggesting anything particularly new or innovative here. Initiating people into Christian discipleship in response to the reign of God has always been at the heart of the mission of the church, even if it was not explicitly described this way.[3] But in order to regenerate evangelism as a missional practice of the church, we need to make a more explicit connection between our wider mission of witness and the narrower mission of evangelism in particular as we consider the three constituents of our witness: outsiders, forgetters, and beloved children.

Let me tell a story of how one forgetter and her beloved child were initiated into Christian discipleship through the witness of the whole church to illustrate the connection I want us to make. It is the story of my mother-in-law, Sandy, and her daughter, my wife, Aisling.

As a young girl growing up in the 1950s, Sandy's parents took her to the Baptist church in Seymour, Indiana, where she remembers sitting in the worship service and staring in awe at the big, bright columns that flowed through the sanctuary. Sandy's grandmother was a strong Christian who read her Bible daily and showed Sandy love, affection, and acceptance. Sandy's parents moved a lot, so they did not always attend church consistently.

But when they settled down in Cincinnati, Ohio, a pastor named Cephas Centers invited her parents to a new church he was starting. Sandy's mom got involved in the church, directing choir, and Sandy went to Sunday school, where she learned the stories of the Bible. She went to the church's summer camp and remembers learning to sing the Doxology. The loving, accepting, and wise ways of a camp counselor had a significant influence on Sandy, and that counselor nurtured in her a sense of wonder at being in God's good creation.

As a preteen, Sandy remembers going to the altar at that church and giving her life to God as the congregation sang, "Just as I Am." The moment she got up from the altar she felt as though a burden had lifted. Soon after, Sandy's grandmother died, and her dad was transferred to Overland Park, Kansas. After the move, the family did not find a church home, and Sandy stopped being a part of a community of witness. Over time the family that had once been part of the church became a family of forgetters. However, Sandy retained a sense of God's presence and remained interested in spiritual things. After graduating from college, she moved to Ireland, where she met and married Martin, with whom she had twin daughters, Aisling and Caoilfhionn. Soon after the girls were born, Sandy and Martin divorced.

Sandy and the girls moved back to the States, back to Overland Park. She remarried and, in 1980, moved into the Nob Hill apartment complex in Kansas City. There, she met Daryll and Verna Stanton, who were students at Nazarene Theological Seminary. Sandy remembers the Stantons as neighbors who were friendly and unassuming. They invited Sandy and her family to their home for dinner. They shared life with them. She doesn't remember them as aggressive or pushy, just real people. The Stantons invited Sandy many times to their church, Kansas City First Church of the Nazarene, and received many refusals from Sandy. Sandy was friendly toward the idea of God but not interested in church. She was put off by organized religion and afraid of cults. By this time in her life, Sandy would be considered a forgetter insofar as she was no longer nurturing her walk with Jesus or participating in the life and mission of God in the world with a Spirit-constituted community of faith.

One day Verna Stanton invited Sandy to a Saturday luncheon drama for women. Sandy went, and was impressed by how much love and acceptance there was from the cast, even when someone messed up a line. Having been involved in drama herself, Sandy expected criticism when the cast made mistakes. But instead she experienced laughter, ease, and joy. The cast members' way of relating to one another was a witness to her. She remembers that as the reason she finally accepted an invitation to attend an Easter sunrise service. Sandy felt a spiritual connection through the congregation's witness of worship at the Easter service. She felt that what was happening there was real to the Stantons, to their pastor, and to the congregation, even if not yet completely for her.

Soon after, Sandy began attending Sunday worship services. A Canadian named Gordon Wetmore was the pastor. He had a limp arm as a result of polio. It was a witness to Sandy to see him preach with a disability. The warmth and welcome of the congregation was also a witness and created a safe space for Sandy to observe their way of being church together. After a few visits, she was relieved to determine that the Church of the Nazarene was not a cult. Sandy began to attend a Sunday school class and met one of the pastors on staff, Charles 'Chic' Shaver. One Sunday, after Sandy had been attending for a while, Chic offered to visit Sandy in her home and talk with her about spiritual things. Sandy took it as an expression of care that he would want to come to her home and talk with her. Her marriage was not going well, her home had become a dark place, and her husband showed violent and dangerous tendencies toward her and her two daughters.

Chic and two others from the church came for a visit. Following the *Evangelism Explosion* script, they shared a plan of salvation with Sandy. When Chic asked Sandy if she would like to accept

Jesus as her Savior, Sandy heard it as an opportunity to renew the commitment to Christ she had made as a child. A forgetter was welcomed home. Because her husband was not receptive, Sandy prayed privately but remembers that, as she prayed, she had what she describes as "a vision of Jesus" over Pastor Shaver. It was a witness of wonder that Sandy took as a sign that she could trust what Chic was asking her to do. From that time forward, Sandy became a regular part of the worshiping community at Kansas City First Church. Her marriage ended soon after, and the church became an important part of the healing that she and her daughters needed. She involved herself in the ministries of the church and, as an adult, reengaged the journey with Jesus that she had left off so many years ago.

Sandy's daughter Aisling immediately became a beloved child of Kansas City First Church. Though she didn't have a father, she gained many loving spiritual fathers who made sure she and her mom and sister were cared for. Aisling doesn't remember having a moment like her mom did, when someone came to her home to invite her to accept Jesus. But she does remember her home being changed through the power of the gospel. Her mother found courage to leave the abusive relationship, and the light of Christ began to shine in their home. Aisling was initiated into Christian discipleship through Sunday school classes, worship services, youth group, summer camps, and the mentorship of spiritually sensitive and mature adults in the church. Over the course of her childhood, youth, and young adult years, she made trips to the altar, asked for and received forgiveness, and consecrated herself to the Lord. She can't name a specific date and time when she accepted Christ; she always remembers being accepted *by* Christ. She was publicly initiated into the Christian church through baptism and profession of faith. The church did not treat Aisling like an outsider or a forgetter; instead, they enfolded her into their loving arms as a beloved child. Through the intentional nurture of the church and its witness of worship, wonder, and way, Aisling now lives as a faithful follower of Jesus.

I share this story of Sandy and Aisling to illustrate how practices of evangelism that are at the heart of our mission of witness do not have to be intrusive, negative, coercive, or pushy, but rather flow from our shared witness of worship, wonder, and way of living in the world. The Stantons were simply being loving neighbors to Sandy. They did not push an agenda but openly shared their way of life. "People need to see how you live your life before they will be receptive. The Stantons were that for me," Sandy remembers. The way the people at the church loved one another and enfolded Sandy and her daughters into that love was witness to her. The regular, weekly worship services at Kansas City First Church also witnessed to Sandy. On Sunday mornings, she observed people who authentically and genuinely worshiped the risen, ascended Jesus, and their witness of worship had an impact on her. As she listened to the sermons and sang the songs, the faith of her childhood was rekindled. The Holy Spirit was wondrously at work in Sandy's life. The awe she experienced in the church of her childhood and the wonder of God's good creation that was cultivated in youth summer camp helped her be attentive to the Spirit when Chic visited her. Because she was a forgetter who had positive memories of church, she welcomed Chic's interest in her spiritual condition when he offered to come to her home.

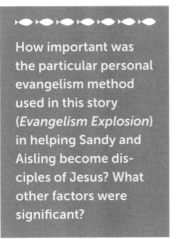

How important was the particular personal evangelism method used in this story (*Evangelism Explosion*) in helping Sandy and Aisling become disciples of Jesus? What other factors were significant?

Aisling's journey into discipleship is different from her mom's. Because of the way the church enfolded her family, Aisling has only known the life and love of Christ through the church. Her Sunday school teachers, pastors, friends, and spiritual mentors all helped initiate her into Christian discipleship. Through baptism, the church signified and celebrated the regenerating work of the Spirit in Aisling's life and her inclusion as a full participant in the life and mission of the church. She has remained a beloved child of the church her whole life.

For the beloved children of the church, evangelism is a ministry of the whole Christian congregation. We are all of us, together, all the time, helping our beloved children, young and old, discover and enter the way of Christian discipleship. At an evangelism workshop, I made the point that evangelism is a ministry of the whole congregation and that part of this ministry includes helping the beloved children of the church mature as disciples of Jesus. After the workshop, an older woman came to me and said something like, "Thank you! This is so helpful. I've spent my whole life ministering to children and youth in the church, but because I've never led anyone in a sinner's prayer, I've never felt like I was doing evangelism. But I have been! I've taught many children and youth about Jesus, prayed with and for them, and encouraged them to follow Jesus. Many of these children are faithful followers of Jesus today." We need to encourage our Sunday school teachers, youth workers, and everyone who works with our children and youth to see how vital their ministry is. They are evangelizing our children through their faithful and often thankless ministries as nursery workers, children's church leaders, Sunday school teachers, summer camp counselors, youth workers (both paid and volunteer), godparents, mentors, and spiritual friends.

Outsiders will likely travel a different path into Christian discipleship than either forgetters or our beloved children. In order to regenerate evangelism as a missional practice of the local church, congregations must be attentive to their unique context. Vancouver is not Kansas City. Forgetters like my mother-in-law, who grew up in a churched culture and carry warm, positive memories of their earlier church experiences are rare in Vancouver and many other global cities today. Many of the evangelism methods developed in the past, such as *Evangelism Explosion, Four Spiritual Laws,* and the *Roman Road* were designed for forgetters who had some previous, positive experience with the church. These methods of evangelism, in effect, said, "Come home" to these forgetters and offered assurance of salvation to those who saw this as their spiritual need.

In my experience with outsiders today, prepared plans of salvation, door knocking, and "come home" methods of evangelism fall flat. When we think about evangelizing outsiders, we need to consider practices of evangelism that have the long view in mind. Evangelizing outsiders would include welcoming them to belong to our community of faith and be involved in our family and community life long before they believe, and certainly before they behave in ways that we might expect Christian disciples to behave. By making space for outsiders to belong before they believe, we graciously offer them an opportunity to glimpse the life of Christian discipleship to which we are calling them, and allowing space for the work of the Spirit to open eyes and unstop ears. This calls us to be faithful in our witness of worship, wonder, and way over the long haul.

In conversation with my fellow pastors in Vancouver, we estimate that it may take around seven years for outsiders who make positive connections with a church to be initiated into Christian discipleship. But in a city like Vancouver with a high rate of mobility, many of the outsiders who come into contact with the church through ministries

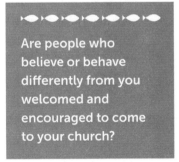

Are people who believe or behave differently from you welcomed and encouraged to come to your church?

such as ESL or refugee services are not around for seven years. In this context, evangelizing outsiders includes the work of gospel-sowing, trusting that the seed that has been planted will grow to maturity even after people move away.

Fiona was a visiting Chinese scholar at the University of British Columbia who, with her family, became part of our community for the months they lived near our church. Fiona befriended the host of our English Conversation Club, a woman named Brenda. Brenda invited Fiona to attend the ladies' Bible study meeting in her home. Over the course of the study, Fiona expressed admiration for the teachings of Jesus and told the ladies in the Bible study that she was trying to put Jesus's teachings into practice in her home and work life. In addition to this, she read the Bible with her family, and her preteen daughter had begun to pray. One evening during the Bible study, Fiona began to speak openly and positively about Jesus. One of the ladies appropriately took the opportunity to ask Fiona if she wanted to accept Jesus into her heart. Fiona refused.

Fiona was either unable or unwilling to respond to the direct invitation to ask Jesus into her heart. She was not interested in joining the Christian religion, which was how she understood the invitation. Yet at the same time, because she had been invited to be part of the ladies' Bible study, she was learning to put Jesus's teachings into practice in her everyday life, and as a result, her life and her whole family were being transformed. Even though she didn't pray to accept Jesus, the ladies in the Bible study were evangelizing Fiona insofar as they were initiating her into Christian discipleship. Through her engagement with our church in a number of different ways, she was discovering what it meant to be a follower of Jesus and put the teachings of Jesus into practice. We do hope that in time, Fiona will come to personal faith in Jesus Christ as a full participant in the life and mission of God in the world. But I am grateful we had the opportunity to help her begin the journey. For Fiona, and many outsiders like her, the journey to Jesus will take time. Our ministries of evangelism to outsiders need to be flexible, creative, patient, and attentive to the work of the Spirit.

Of course, repentance and faith are necessary for full initiation into Christian discipleship. The good news of God's reign calls for a response. In Acts 2, following the wonder of the Pentecost event and Peter's words of wonder, the people are "cut to the heart" (Acts 2:37) and ask Peter what they should do.

Peter replied, "Repent and be baptized, every one of you, in the name of Jesus Christ for the forgiveness of your sins. And you will receive the gift of the Holy Spirit. The promise is for you and your children and for all who are far off—for all whom the Lord our God will call." ...Those who accepted his message were baptized, and about three thousand were added to their number that day.

Acts 2:38-39, 41

It is this call to repentance and faith in Jesus that often causes conflict between the church and the world. We cannot ignore or be naïve to the challenge that the witness and evangelism of the church bring to the world. People may appreciate our witness of our worship, wonder, and way and still not want to be initiated into Christian discipleship in response to the reign of God. Regenerating evangelism as a missional practice of the church means we take seriously the biblical truth that evangelism includes a summons to a new allegiance and incorporation into the new community of the Holy Spirit that seeks to live as witness to the reign of God through its worship, wonder, and way. Beloved children, forgetters, and outsiders need to be invited to receive Jesus and become his disciples. They may need guidance on how to repent, and what to believe. Evangelism is intended to initiate persons into Christian discipleship, and without intention on the part of the Christian community, evangelism will not happen.

We use the word *conversion* to describe the change of heart, mind, will, and attitude that is a central part of what it means to receive Jesus as Savior

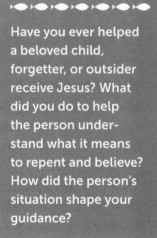

Have you ever helped a beloved child, forgetter, or outsider receive Jesus? What did you do to help the person understand what it means to repent and believe? How did the person's situation shape your guidance?

and Lord. Conversion is a biblical word used to describe what happens when persons are initiated into discipleship in response to the reign of God in Christ. Whether a person's conversion takes place in a moment of crisis or as a longer process, the twofold response required by Peter in his sermon in Acts 2 remains at the heart of the conversion experience that signifies a person's turning away from the kingdoms of this world and turning toward the kingdom of God.

This twofold response is repentance and baptism: "Repent and be baptized, every one of you, in the name of Jesus Christ for the forgiveness of your sins. And you will receive the gift of the Holy Spirit. The promise is for you and your children and for all who are far off—for all whom the Lord our God will call" (Acts 2:38-39). In the book of Acts, repentance and baptism are inseparable from participation in the life and mission of the Christian church.

Through baptism we are commissioned into the mission of God for the life of the world. To be baptized is to become a member of the Spirit-empowered witnessing community. All who are baptized into fellowship with Christ and his church are now witnesses and, together, have the great joy and privilege of helping initiate beloved children, forgetters, and outsiders into Christian discipleship in response to the reign of God. We bear witness to this reign through our worship, wonder, and way. And we lovingly seek to initiate everyone who calls on the name of the Lord into discipleship, baptizing them in the name of the Father and of the Son and of the Holy Spirit, and teaching them to obey everything Jesus commanded. Jesus has promised to be with us always as we carry out this commission, to the very end of the age.

Evangelism is the heart of our mission of witness. As you engage this mission with your congregation in the places you live and move and work and pray and play in these days, I pray you will do so with Spirit-empowered confidence and Spirit-filled joy, in love, for the life of the world.

6 ⬤ Personal Evangelism: Prayer

Acts 4:31: After they prayed, the place where they were meeting was shaken. And they were all filled with the Holy Spirit and spoke the word of God boldly.

A recent report published by the Barna Group asked the question: *Is evangelism going out of style?* According to their study, 73 percent of people who identify as born-again Christians in North America agree that they have a *personal* responsibility to share their Christian faith with others. However, in practice, the research shows that evangelism *is on the decline* among nearly two out of three active Christians today. The bottom line is that millions of Christians remain committed to the *idea* of evangelism but don't act on that conviction.[1]

This research confirms the experience of many pastors and churches in world areas where Christianity has been established for generations. Most churchgoers feel they should be doing personal evangelism, but few are actually doing what they think they should be doing. The noticeable gap between conviction and action makes many people feel bad.

I am very interested in why people don't act on their conviction. And what I've come to realize is that one of the reasons many Christians today don't actually engage in evangelism is that they associate evangelism with a set of practices, behaviors, or approaches by which *they themselves* are turned off and with which they don't want to be associated. For many people, personal evangelism does not seem very personal.

For example, some people think personal evangelism is knocking on strangers' doors to tell them about Jesus, which is not very personal at all. When a stranger knocks on my door to sell me a product or promote a religion, I don't like that. I consider it an invasion of my privacy and not very respectful of me as a person. I've seen personal evangelism practiced as setting up a meeting with someone and going into that conversation with a pre-planned script in which one maneuvers the conversation in such a way as to get the person to agree with one's religious beliefs through logical argumentation, *gotcha* questions, and pressure techniques. These practices are not very personal either. I don't like conversations where I feel like someone is pitching something to me. I've seen personal evangelism practiced as seeking to build a relationship with someone who is considered unsaved—not because one is actually interested in getting to know the person or learn about that person's background and life experiences but only with the goal of sharing one's religious beliefs with that person. And if they are not responsive, the relationship is dropped like a hot potato. That is *not* personal. I don't like to feel like I am someone's project, and that a person's only interest in me is getting me to conform to their belief or opinion. Our practices of evangelism need to be personal.

Evangelism is personal because God's very being is personal: Father, Son, and Holy Spirit. And our personal God desires above all else to draw *persons* into God's triune life, setting *persons* free from the depersonalizing effects of sin and death; initiating *persons* into the life and love of God through repentance and faith in Jesus Christ; restoring the image of God in *persons*; and welcoming *persons* into the new community of the Spirit where we become part of the family of God. The triune God created people to inhabit this world because God's being is personal, and God loves people! The church's ministries of evangelism must reflect the personal nature of God.

In a Facebook post, my friend Daron shared how a church took a *personal* interest in his family that changed his life:

> It began when I was 10 years old—the oldest of 3 kids to a single mother. We were broken in more ways than we realized. A local Church of the Nazarene in Clarksville, Tennessee, sought us, welcomed us, and loved us toward wholeness and healing.

What a beautiful testimony to the redemptive power of a loving congregation. This is evangelism that is personal.

This was Jesus's way of evangelism. Jesus's way of evangelism was personal because the goal of his evangelism was to invite people to *personally* become his followers; to *personally* join his company of disciples. Jesus didn't ask people to join his religion but, rather, to join themselves personally to *him*. Don't ever lose sight of the fact that Jesus's goal, during his three-year ministry on earth, was to gather women and men to *himself*; to invite them into a personal relationship with him as his disciples. Everywhere he went, Jesus invited people to follow him. He did this knowing that, through his sacrificial death on the cross, he would *ransom* their very lives, claiming them as his own, setting them free from the scourge of sin and the person-destroying catastrophe of death. After his resurrection and ascension, Jesus gave his disciples the gift of the person of the Holy Spirit, who would bind them together as a new community of people—men and women drawn from all

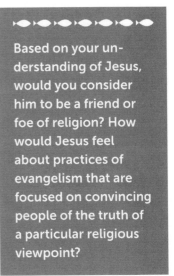

Based on your understanding of Jesus, would you consider him to be a friend or foe of religion? How would Jesus feel about practices of evangelism that are focused on convincing people of the truth of a particular religious viewpoint?

walks of life who would now journey together in this world as witnesses to Jesus, drawing other persons into fellowship with Jesus through the fellowship of the church, through their life together in the world.

Evangelism that is personal is evangelism that is characterized by a Jesus-like, loving concern for persons to belong to the new community of Jesus disciples, to become disciples of Jesus who are:

- healed from the scourge and forgiven of the guilt of sin;
- recipients of eternal life, sons and daughters of God, people over whom death no longer holds sway;
- followers of Jesus who worship the Father through him; experience the wondrous power and presence of the Holy Spirit in their life together; and walk in the ways of Jesus, doing justice, loving mercy, and walking humbly with Jesus and their fellow disciples in the world;
- united with Christ through faith; participants of the divine nature living in joyous union with the Father, Son, and Holy Spirit.

What practices does evangelism that is personal involve? Everyone can *personally* participate in evangelism that is personal by *personally* engaging in three *personal* practices. These include:

1. Personal prayer for people (Chapter 6)
2. Sharing personal stories with people (Chapter 7)
3. Going on personal journeys with people (Chapter 8)

Evangelism in the early church is characterized by passionate, personal prayer. In Acts 4:23-31, we catch a glimpse of a prayer meeting in the early church. This passage immediately follows

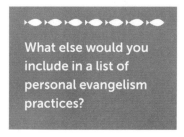

What else would you include in a list of personal evangelism practices?

the story of Peter and John, two of Jesus's disciples, who heal a man who was crippled from birth. The healing of the man in Jesus's name creates quite a stir in Jerusalem (witness of wonder). The preaching of the disciples on the heels of this healing threatens the ruling powers, who only recently colluded with King Herod and the Roman governor, Pontius Pilate, to put Jesus to death! But, as we know from the story, Jesus isn't dead. God raised him from the dead. Jesus has now ascended to the right hand of God the Father and poured out the Holy Spirit on the disciples, empowering them for their mission of witness in the world. The rulers and authorities in Jerusalem don't want this witness to continue. So they drag Peter and John into court and order them to stop healing and teaching in Jesus's name. These threats against Peter and John and the other disciples are real. Throughout history, the powers of this world have stood against the healing, liberating power of the kingdom of God. In many parts of our world today, there is a lot of hostility against any Christian church or any Christian person who publicly makes Christ known or seeks to help women and men, young and old become followers of Jesus.

An editorialist in the *Vancouver Courier* recently accused a church plant in the city of holding values antithetical to Canadian multiculturalism because they seek to help people become followers of Jesus. Make no mistake; we live in a world that is not friendly toward the ministry and message of Jesus. We live in a world that resists God's claim on people's lives and is indifferent or hostile to Jesus's call to follow him. We might be tempted to gather as a holy huddle, circle the wagons, fill up our savings accounts, and try to hold out for as long as possible until Jesus returns. But that is not our mission! Our mission is to bear public witness to the reign of God through our worship, wonder, and way of living in the world, and to engage in loving, intentional activities governed by the goal of initiating people into discipleship to Jesus. We can't do this on our own or under our own power. We were never intended to. The disciples in Acts 4 know they can't do it on their own. They know they need God's help. So they raise their voices to God in prayer.

Evangelism that is personal begins with personal prayer to a very personal God for the persons with whom we are in personal relationships. We pray for people we are personally involved with on their journeys to becoming disciples of Jesus. Begin with five people in your circle of relationships, what I've heard called your "high-five list." Here is the *first* practice of evangelism that is personal: Pray for five people you are in personal relationships with whom you hope will become disciples of Jesus. Consider a mix of five people that includes: beloved children, forgetters, and outsiders.

As a father, the first two names on my high-five list are my boys. My sons are already well on the journey of Christian discipleship. They have both professed faith in Jesus Christ and have been initiated into Christian discipleship through baptism. But I know from my own experience, growing up in a Christian home, that the faith journey of beloved children goes through many stages. Praying a prayer to accept Jesus and being baptized is only the beginning of Christian discipleship; it is not the end. I want to persist in personal prayer for my beloved sons that they will become mature followers of Jesus; united to Christ in faith, hope, and love; and share in the mission of God in the world within the context of a vibrant community of faith.

Pray personally for forgetters. In my years as a pastor, I was aware of people who passed through the congregation with whom we lost touch. Some of these are our beloved children who disconnected from the worshiping life of our congregation and haven't found a home elsewhere. Some are women and men who were moving toward Christ but whose journey has been frustrated or derailed for one reason or another. Do you know any forgetters? Pray personal prayers for the women and men you know whose journeys of faith have been stunted, derailed, or frustrated.

Are you friends with any outsiders? If not, you might need to pray first for the Holy Spirit to move you out of your comfort zone and into relationships with those who are not currently disciples of Jesus. There is no shortage of outsiders in Vancouver. As a church, we were blessed to be in regular personal relationships with outsiders who were new to Canada through our ESL program and our English Conversation Club. In my neighborhood, most of my Canadian friends were outsiders to Christian disciple-ship. Jesus took a personal interest in outsiders, and so should his disciples today. First, pray for the Holy Spirit to illuminate the person. If you are looking for specific words to use, a great prayer to pray for the people on your high-five list is Paul's prayer in Ephesians 1:17-19a:

I keep asking that the God of our Lord Jesus Christ, the glorious Father, may give you the Spirit of wisdom and revelation, so that you may know him better. I pray that the eyes of your heart may be enlightened in order that you may know the hope to which he has called you, the riches of his glorious inheritance in his holy people, and his incomparably great power for us who believe.

John Dickson calls this kind of prayer "the hidden mission" of evangelism. Praying for the Spirit to illuminate the people on your high-five list *is* evangelism that is personal. "Not all of us will feel confident speaking to others about salvation, but all of us can be confident speaking about others to the Saviour himself," writes Dickson.[2]

Second, pray for doors to be opened in your relationships with the people on your high-five list so you will have opportunities to share the hope you have in Jesus. This is how the apostle Paul asks the church in Colossae to pray for him in Colossians 4:3: "And pray for us, too, that God may open a door for our message, so that we may proclaim the mystery of Christ, for which I am in chains." One of the ways God opens doors in people's lives for the message of Jesus in the book of Acts is through signs and wonders. In Acts 4:30, the disciples call out to God, asking God to "stretch out your hand to heal and perform signs and wonders through the name of your holy servant Jesus." It could be that some of the people on your high-five list are facing a difficulty or a challenge in life that is too great for them to handle alone. Praying for doors to be opened might include praying for their healing; praying for the resolution to a difficult situation; praying for them for God's guidance or encouragement or power to be revealed in such a way that it opens a door for you to share about the hope you have in Jesus Christ.

We were reflecting on Acts 4:23-31 in a Wednesday prayer group. One of the participants shared how she recently had been invited to a friend's home for dinner. Her friend could be considered a forgetter, a person raised in a nominal Christian environment, who knows the basics of the Christian story, but is not living as an active disciple of Jesus. This person shared that she had been praying for an open door to witness to Jesus. She said that at dinner that night, much to her surprise, her friend asked her if she would pray a New Year's blessing over her. She was so surprised that this friend asked her to pray in this way. But then she remembered that this was an answer to her prayer for an open door. She prayed for the Lord to bless her friend in the new year, and she continues to pray that this friend will come to see that the blessings of her life are gifts of God's grace and signs of God's personal love.

Third, pray for courage to speak when appropriate. In Acts 4:29, the disciples ask the Lord for the ability to speak "with great boldness." Sometimes we make the mistake of believing that all of Jesus's disciples and the early apostles, like Paul and Barnabas, were naturally courageous and fearless. But it's not true.
Paul frequently asks people to pray for him. I have no doubt that there are many times when Paul is timid and afraid. He prays for courage. So too do we need to ask for courage to talk about Jesus, whether it is a conversation around the dinner table with your beloved children, a phone call to a forgetter you haven't seen for a while, or over coffee with an outsider you've been praying for.

I remember one of the first friends I ever talked to in a personal way about Jesus. His name was Mike. Mike was in a karate class with me. The karate instructor was a Christian, as well as another guy in the class, and we prayed together that Mike would come to know Jesus. It was actually kind of weird to be throwing punches at a guy I was praying for, but he was a higher belt than I was, so he hit me more often than I hit him. When you are praying for boldness and courage to speak to someone about Jesus, it affects your relationship with that person. You begin to wonder when and how God is going to answer your prayer. You listen for things that might reveal a person's openness to Jesus. You get a little bold in your conversation with that person about your own spiritual journey. One day Mike asked me a question about my faith that opened a door to a larger conversation about Jesus. By the end of that conversation, Mike expressed an interest in knowing Jesus personally and becoming his follower. It all began with prayer—three guys in a karate studio, praying personally for our friend Mike.

> Can you recall a time in your life when you felt emboldened to talk about Jesus with someone? What was that experience like?

Fourth, pray for clarity of words. Many Christians express concern that they do not know how to talk about Jesus. Before you worry about *what* to say, I encourage you to pray for the Spirit to *give* you clarity of words when the door to speak opens. The first disciples of Jesus encourage new disciples to be prepared to talk about Jesus. In 1 Peter 3:15, Peter writes: "Always be prepared to give an answer to everyone who asks you to give the reason for the hope that you have." But preparing to speak does not necessarily mean memorizing a speech. The first preparation of evangelism that is personal is the preparation of prayer, asking for the Lord's help in *what* to say and *how* to say it.

Jesus promises to help his disciples speak on his behalf. In Luke 12:11-12, Jesus says to his disciples: "When you are brought before synagogues, rulers and authorities, do not worry about how you will defend yourselves or what you will say, for the Holy Spirit will teach you at that time what you should say." The Lord keeps this promise, and when Peter and John are brought before the rulers and authorities in Acts 4, Peter, filled with the Holy Spirit, finds just the right words to speak. You don't need to be ordained or receive a doctorate in evangelism to be able to speak clearly about Jesus. The first disciples are regular and unschooled women and men. We do need the preparation of prayer, and the power of the Holy Spirit, and the personal experience of being followers of Jesus ourselves. Pray for the Spirit to give you clarity of words when it is time to speak.

Fifth, pray for an increase of love, both for the person you are praying for, and for that person's awareness of how much God loves him or her. Evangelism that is personal begins in prayer that is rooted in love. A very practical prayer to pray for your high-five is Paul's prayer in Ephesians 3:16-19:

> I pray that out of his glorious riches [the Father] may strengthen you with power through his Spirit in your inner being, so that Christ may dwell in your hearts through faith. And I pray that you, being rooted and established in love, may have power, together with all the Lord's holy people, to grasp how wide and long and high and deep is the love of Christ, and to know this love that surpasses knowledge—that you may be filled to the measure of all the fullness of God.

Pray the name of someone on your high-five list in this scripture: *"I pray that _____ may grasp how wide and long and high and deep is the love of Christ."*

God loves the people on your high-five list. God wants everyone to be brought into the loving fellowship of Father, Son, and Holy Spirit. If we want our practices of evangelism to be personal, we need to be drawn into that fellowship of divine love as well, which is the only proper motivation for our evangelistic witness in the world.

Most Christians believe they are supposed to share their faith with others. Few Christians actually do. We don't feel good about this discrepancy because we love our family and friends, we know God loves them, and we want them to know God's love. We can begin to close the gap between our aspiration and our actual practice by simply beginning with prayer. Praying these five prayers for each person on your high-five list *is* evangelism that is personal.

7 Personal Evangelism: Stories

Acts 5:20: *"Go, stand in the temple courts," he said, "and tell the people all about this new life."*

Doug drives an airport shuttle bus in Vancouver. He recently shared with me about how he is engaging in personal prayer for his boss, a man from Singapore named Ray. "I don't personally interact with my boss very often," Doug explained, "but about a week ago during some down time, Ray started talking to me about some of the stresses of his work and the medical concerns that are related to his stress."

In the context of that conversation Doug said to his boss: "Ray, I want you to know that I am praying for you and for your company."

Ray had his back to him, but when Doug told him he was praying for him, Ray turned around slowly, and after a reflective pause, looked Doug in the eye and said: "Doug, I want you to know how much I appreciate that."

Two days later, Doug and Ray were driving together on business for the company. In the flow of the conversation, Doug shared with Ray his plan to use the tips he received from driving the shuttle bus to fund a well in Bangladesh through Nazarene Compassionate Ministries. This intrigued Ray, who asked Doug about his life, which opened a door for Doug to share his personal story about his journey with Jesus and the joy he has found in participating in God's works of mercy and compassion around the world.

Doug began with personal prayer; when asked, he took the opportunity to share his personal story about his journey with Jesus. Evangelism that is personal includes sharing personal stories with the people we are praying for. Evangelism stands at the front end of the lifelong journey of Christian discipleship. Evangelism is lovingly helping people become followers of Jesus. Most people come to know about who Jesus is and what Jesus came to do through the words of Jesus's followers.

In Acts 5:42 we learn about the witness of the first followers of Jesus in Jerusalem: "Day after day, in the temple courts and from house to house, they never stopped teaching and proclaiming the good news that Jesus is the Messiah." This verse leaves me with the impression that talking about Jesus is as natural as part of the lives of these early Christians as talking about the Vancouver Canuck hockey team is to people living in Vancouver. In their homes, in their places of worship, in their normal, day-to-day activities, they never stop sharing personal stories of their experience with the risen, living Lord.

When it comes to speaking about Jesus to our beloved children, forgetters, and outsiders, there are some in every Christian congregation who seem to be wonderfully gifted by the Holy Spirit with the ability to talk about Jesus in such a way that is effective in drawing others to faith in Jesus Christ. In the New Testament, these are the people who are said to have "the gift of the evangelist." New Testament scholar John Dickson finds that the word *evangelist* was actually created by the first Christians "as a shorthand way of referring to those in the church who took on the task of proclaiming the life, death and resurrection of God's Messiah to those for whom this message was *still news*."[1]

My mentor and friend, Dr. Charles 'Chic' Shaver has the gift of the evangelist. Chic has an acute desire to share Jesus with others. He relates well to forgetters and outsiders. While picking up his mail from the community mailbox, Chic once noticed a man setting up a camera. He struck up a conversation and discovered that the man was a student from Princeton who was conducting a research project on mail-delivery systems. Chic, who graduated from Dartmouth, another Ivy League school, engaged the man in a conversation and ended up sharing with him the story of how Jesus Christ changed his life when he was a law student at Dartmouth. The man found Chic's story so compelling that he asked if he could film it and share it with others. Chic has the gift of the evangelist!

But not every Christian has the gift of the evangelist, just as not every Christian has gifts of teaching, administration, healing, prophecy, or service. However, it seems that in the last half of the twentieth century, with the rise of television and radio, and media-centered Christianity, those with the gift of the evangelist gained such prominence in the church that they became the model of what Christian believed we are all supposed to be.

When I ask people what image comes to their mind when they hear the word *evangelism*, they frequently mention Billy Graham. But not every Christian can do what Billy Graham did or what Chic Shaver does. And if Christians think they have to do what Billy Graham or Chic Shaver does in order to practice evangelism, it's no wonder so many Christians do not consider themselves competent to practice evangelism. We do not all have the gift of the evangelist. But with God's help, we can do some of the work of the evangelist—that is, we can go public with the story of Jesus within the sphere of our personal relationships, helping people on the first steps of becoming followers of Jesus.

In his book *Evangelism in the Early Church*, Michael Green suggests that it was the "informal evangelists" who were most responsible for spreading the Christian faith.[2] They did so through their normal social networks, sharing the hope they had in Jesus Christ with the people they were in personal relationships with. Most Christians are informal evangelists. We cannot imagine ourselves striking up conversations with strangers at mailboxes, but we could imagine ourselves talking personally with our children, family, friends, neighbors, or coworkers about our journey with Jesus and the hope we have found in Jesus Christ.

> Would you be comfortable thinking of yourself as an informal evangelist? What personal qualities do you think would be important for an informal evangelist to have?

Peter encourages every Christian in the churches under his care to be prepared and willing to give an account of the hope they have in Jesus Christ, and to do so with gentleness and respect. How do we prepare ourselves to give an account of the hope we have in Jesus Christ today?

1. Rehearse the big story.
2. Rehearse Jesus's story.
3. Rehearse your story.

First, rehearse the big story. The big story is basically a summary of the whole story of the Bible from Genesis to Revelation, from creation to the new creation, with Jesus Christ as the centerpiece and focal point. This big story begins with God's creational intention to develop the world as a place of blessing, a meeting place for God and God's creation. Made in God's image, people are given the task of stewarding the earth and its resources for the common good. The people God creates disregard their Creator and seek to develop life apart from God. Cut off from God's blessing because of their sin, people become estranged from God, from God's creation, and from one another.

But God does not give up on the people or the world God created; instead, God gets involved in the healing and restoration of the world. God blesses a family (Abraham), and a people (Israel), setting them apart and sending them into the world as a holy people to represent and embody God's creational intention for the whole human race. Through Israel, God's blessing will come to all the peoples of the earth and the whole creation itself. When these people fall short of their missional vocation, God forgives and restores them, sending them prophets, priests, and kings to remind them whose they are and to chasten them. God remains faithful to God's covenant promises, even when the people are unfaithful.

God's plan to redeem, renew, and restore all things comes to fulfillment when God moves into the neighborhood through Jesus Christ. Indwelt and empowered by the Holy Spirit, Jesus faithfully fulfills Israel's missional vocation. At the cross, Jesus makes full atonement for the whole human race. Through the resurrection, Jesus disarms and defeats the powers of sin and death. At his ascension, Jesus returns to the Father's right hand then pours out the Holy Spirit, by which a new people are created to extend the mission of God to the very ends of the earth. As witnesses to the rescuing, redeeming, and restoring mission of God, the church is sent as a holy people in the power of the Spirit, representing and embodying God's creational intention for the whole human race.

There are many other ways to tell this big story that stay true to the biblical narrative. Find a way that works for you and practice telling and retelling it. Try to get to a point where it is as concise as you can make it while still making sense in your context.

When the early Christians teach and preach in Jerusalem, they do so in a context in which their Jewish friends, family, and neighbors are familiar with the broad outlines of this big story, from creation to God's interventions through Israel to the expectation of God's return to set things right again.

▶◆▶◆▶◆▶◆▶◆▶◆▶◆

How would you tell the big story? What part of the big story is the most compelling to you? What part of the big story gets the most emphasis in your church?

It is within the broader context of this big story that their preaching of Jesus Christ makes sense. Today, the case remains the same. Terms like *Christ* or *Messiah, kingdom of God, repentance,* and *sin* only make sense in the context of the big story. The good news that Jesus is the Christ only makes sense, and only feels like good news, if one is already at least a little familiar with the big story, including Israel's hope that God would send his Messiah to save people from their sin and set the world right again.

If you grew up in North America in the twentieth century, you probably learned parts of the big story simply through living in a culture that was friendly and familiar with the story and that retold parts of this big story in public ways. This prevalence of the story is not the case anymore. In many parts of North America, people are no longer familiar with the big story. Sadly, even many Christians today are not familiar with the big story. We live in world of false stories, half-truths, and deceptions. My boys are growing up in an education system that seeks to convince them "that [their] destiny and happiness is to be found in...turning to a bold use of [their own] resources to solve [their] problems."[3] I live in a world that constantly invites me "to find [my] true welfare in an endless round of pleasure and happiness."[4] The purpose of life in this story is to retire with more than a million dollars in the bank so I can enjoy the final years of my life.

We all live in a world that tells us that might makes right; suffering is an illusion; people get what they deserve; the material world is all there is; and self-fulfillment is the ultimate aim of human existence. Christians live by a different story, however. Christians believe that in the life, death, resurrection, and ascension of Jesus, a new world has been opened up to us; a new vision for living is possible; a new story is being told that is a far more compelling and attractive and hope-filled story than any of the stories by which we currently live our lives. Evangelism that is personal is rooted in sharing personal stories that are shaped by and flow from this big story.

There are a number of books being published these days that promote this big story in fresh and compelling ways, including books by Christian authors such as NT Wright, Christopher

Wright, and Scot McKnight. Sharing Christian literature with your friends is one way to get the big story in their hands. One of the books I've given to friends of mine who are outsiders is a book by NT Wright called *Simply Christian* that does a good job of telling the big story in a way that is accessible today.

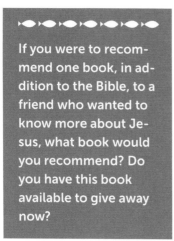

If you were to recommend one book, in addition to the Bible, to a friend who wanted to know more about Jesus, what book would you recommend? Do you have this book available to give away now?

It is important that our beloved children come to learn and know this story. The beloved children of the church get to know the big story through songs, scriptures, and preaching in the worship of the church. In Sunday school classes, children's church, small groups, and summer camps, they can engage the big story in creative ways. In the bedtime stories and table talk in our homes, we have opportunities to continually tell and retell and rehearse the big story with our children, youth, and one another.

Forgetters need to be reminded of the big story. The lost son in Luke 15 comes to his senses when he remembers his father's house and the generosity of his father. He comes to realize that the story he has been living by—the story of conspicuous consumption and a frenetic pursuit of pleasure—is bankrupt. When he comes to his senses, he remembers that his father is compassionate and merciful, slow to anger and quick to forgive. The son returns home and finds a way of living that is characterized by mercy and forgiveness, a hope-filled, life-giving, and generative way of life.

Outsiders may not even know that such an alternative story exists. A friend of mine in Seattle once shared that his dad taught him that all there is to life is the material possessions of this world. And when you die, they put your body in the ground and that's the end. So eat, drink, and be merry, for tomorrow you may die. That was the story by which he lived. I remember the day that man was baptized in Lake Washington. He was baptized into a new story, a resurrection story. Through the witness of our church in Seattle and the sharing of our personal stories with him, this man came to realize that his dad's story was tragically misinformed. Death is not the final word; life is!

The big story is about a God who loves and creates life, who redeems and recreates life, the Lord and life-giver, who desires life for all people everywhere. Evangelism that is personal is rooted in the big story of this personal God.

Rehearse this big story. Share this big story. We do this not simply because we are trying to win people to our story but because, as Thomas Long writes in his book *Testimony: Talking Ourselves into Being Christian*: "At the most profound level, Christians talk about faith because it is a truly human act to want to tell the truth."[5]

Second, evangelism that is personal is centered on Jesus's story. The big story has Jesus as its main character. In Acts 5:42 it says "they never stopped teaching and proclaiming the good news that Jesus is the Messiah." This is a very focused and specific message that is at the heart of the big story. It is what we call the gospel.

In the New Testament, the gospel—or, good news—that Jesus is the Christ has specific content. The best way to familiarize yourself with the core content of the gospel is to read the Gospels; to study the apostolic preaching in the book of Acts; and to familiarize yourself with Paul's summaries of the gospel in his letters. This is more reading than you can probably do in one day, one week, or even one month. But if you want to learn how to share the story of Jesus, you must first get to know the story of Jesus and familiarize yourself with summaries of his story as told in the New Testament. Immersing yourself in these stories is the best way to prepare yourself to give an account of the hope you have in Jesus Christ.[6]

When sharing stories about Jesus with our beloved children, forgetters, and outsiders, John Dickson suggests we think about sharing what he calls "gospel-bites" when appropriate. Dickson is aware that for those of us without the gift of the evangelist, it is probably unlikely that we will have many opportunities to share the whole story of Jesus with people in one sitting. But we can share gospel-bites, a practice that involves involves retelling a brief episode from Jesus's life (a conversation, a miracle, a parable, whatever) that in some way connects to a conversation, question, or life situation that comes up in our everyday interactions.

Someone who does this naturally is my friend Brian Postlewait, executive director of Mission Possible, a Nazarene Compassionate Ministry working to end street homelessness in Vancouver's notorious downtown eastside. Brian would not say he has the gift of the evangelist. But in conversations with street workers and business leaders, he frequently shares gospel-bites, a bit of the story of Jesus in a way that connects the story of Jesus to the work of Mission Possible in a way that witnesses to Jesus. Brian doesn't transmit the whole big picture or the whole account of Jesus in every conversation, but I am always impressed by the way he alludes to the big story and weaves gospel-bites into his conversations.

My friend Brenda does this as well. Brenda would not consider herself an evangelist, but I used to eavesdrop on Brenda when she talked with people at the English Conversation Club she led at the church. She often shared gospel-bites with the people she built relationships with. It never felt forced or awkward; it just flowed as a natural part of her conversations. This is evangelism that is personal.

Rehearse Jesus's story. Familiarize yourself with the gospel. Share gospel-bites when appropriate. Finally, rehearse *your* story. So much of our lives are lived in sharing others' experiences. We trust our friends' opinions and evaluations, the analyses of our family members in trivial matters such as consumer product satisfaction and where to get a good meal, and they trust us in return—so why not in a matter as significant as how the gospel has transformed our lives?

In our church in Seattle, there was a woman named Ms. Mary. Ms. Mary always wore a huge, diamond-studded pin on her blouse that said *Jesus*. Frequently during our church services, Ms. Mary would stand up, literally take over the service, and share how God had been at work in her life over the past week. Ms. Mary worked among children at risk in some of the most dangerous and poverty-stricken areas of Seattle, so most of the time her stories were riveting tales of how God had miraculously intervened in the midst of a terrible situation to bring hope and healing to the lives of the children she loved. Her personal stories of experiences with Jesus were a powerful witness to the presence of the living Jesus in the world.

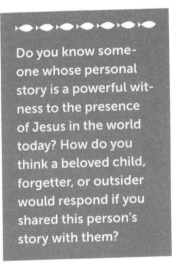

Do you know someone whose personal story is a powerful witness to the presence of Jesus in the world today? How do you think a beloved child, forgetter, or outsider would respond if you shared this person's story with them?

In spiritual formation groups, I encourage participants to reflect on their lives since the last time the group met and share one way they have experienced the leading, help, or presence of the Holy Spirit. While not every story is as dramatic as Ms. Mary's, I am always amazed at the power of a personal story when a person opens up and shares the ways that Jesus is at work in his or her life.

I was taught that a personal testimony had to have three parts:

1. Describe my life before I put my faith in Jesus Christ;
2. Describe when and where I received Christ and prayed a sinner's prayer;
3. Describe the difference that faith in Christ has made in my life.

What is interesting to notice is that people who are taught to share their testimony this way are often beloved children of the church. Beloved children often cannot remember a time in their life before they put their faith in Jesus; they have known Jesus since they were children! As a result of twisting their stories to conform to this outline, their so-called personal testimonies don't end up sounding very personal at all. They often feel forced, contrived, canned. Evangelism that is personal involves sharing personal stories that highlight the significance of Jesus Christ in your life *as it actually happens*, not forcing your stories to conform to someone else's pattern.

In his book *Transforming Conversion*, Gordon Smith encourages Christians to write out and rehearse their spiritual autobiographies, by which he means describing what has *actually* happened and is *actually* happening in your life as a consequence of your personal relationship with Jesus Christ. Take time to reflect on and rehearse how the person and work of Jesus Christ has influenced, transformed, directed, revolutionized or shaped your life today, focusing on the aspects of Jesus's personhood that have affected you the most. The three aspects of his ministry were Jesus as prophet, priest, and king. But you could also use teacher, forgiver, or healer if you like, or another set of words that somehow captures the central aspects of Jesus's life and ministry, and how they have touched your own life. Jesus was the greatest teacher who ever lived. Jesus is the source of our restored awareness of the big story. When you share personal stories with our beloved children, forgetters, and outsiders, share how Jesus's teachings and vision of the kingdom of God have shaped your life.

At the core of many people's experience of Jesus is the personal reception of his offer of forgiveness of sin. At the center of the gospel message is the cross. Jesus is our great high priest, our forgiver. Jesus is the one who, by taking the guilt of our sin upon himself, makes possible our reconciliation to God and maintains us in that relationship. When you share personal stories with our beloved children, forgetters, and outsiders, share personally how receiving the forgiveness and reconciliation offered by Jesus has shaped your life.

Jesus is the risen, ascended Lord, the King who reigns today. It is only through the grace and power of Christ our King that we are able to live as his disciples today. As King, Jesus is the hope and desire of all the nations. Jesus is the one who is making all things new, the healer and restorer of life. Through Jesus our healer, the image of God is graciously restored in us, and we become children of God. When you share personal stories with our beloved children, forgetters, and outsiders, share personally how Jesus is healing and restoring you, and how your hope in Christ's restoration of all things brings you hope today.

If you are interested in engaging in practices of evangelism that are personal, begin by rehearsing the big story; then rehearse Jesus's story; and, finally, rehearse your story, in light of the big story and Jesus's story. As you do so, you will be "prepared to give the reason for the hope that you have" in Jesus Christ (1 Peter 3:15). Sharing personal stories is evangelism that is personal.

8 ⚬ Personal Evangelism: Journey

Acts 8:36: As they traveled along the road, they came to some water and the eunuch said, "Look, here is water. What can stand in the way of my being baptized?"

Philip is one of the first people in the New Testament to be called an evangelist. Philip is not one of Jesus's original twelve disciples. He is a second-generation follower of Jesus, someone who has come to faith in Jesus through the witness of the apostles. Philip may never have met Jesus personally. He is a Greek-speaking Jewish follower of Jesus, whose family has likely migrated from their original homeland in Palestine to another part of the Greek-speaking world. At some point in his life, Philip returned to Jerusalem, and there he first hears the good news of Jesus Christ and becomes a follower of Jesus.

Philip makes his first appearance in Acts chapter 6, where he is chosen by the apostles to help oversee the daily distribution of food to the poor. I've known many followers of Jesus whose first ministry experience was volunteering in a compassionate ministry center, serving meals or sorting clothing. It appears to be through Philip's ministry of compassion, participating in the church's witness of way, that he grows and develops as a disciple of Jesus.

When persecution drives Philip out of Jerusalem, he moves to Samaria and begins making disciples there. Then, during what seems to be a time of prayer, the LORD inspires Philip to join a group of travelers heading down the desert highway to Egypt.

Luke doesn't tell us, but I suspect that Philip and the Ethiopian have met before. After all, Philip is a Greek-speaking Jew who evidently travels widely. I suspect he may have lived in Alexandria, Egypt, and perhaps was involved in some sort of administrative position there since he is recognized by the apostles as having administrative skills. The Ethiopian eunuch is an important official in charge of all the treasury of the queen of the Ethiopians. Perhaps Philip has been involved in some business dealings with him in the past. I doubt this official would just invite any old hitchhiker into his carriage with him. I can picture Philip walking in the midst of the herd of travelers on the desert highway, scanning the crowd for a familiar face, attentive to the leading of the Spirit. On the way the Spirit prompts Philip, saying, *Go and join the man in the chariot*. In the NIV it is translated: "Go and stay near" the chariot.

Once you know the whole story, you can see the full intent of the Spirit in this brief command. The intent of the Spirit is for Philip to get in the chariot and go on a journey with this man; to go all the way to Jesus with him, all the way to his baptism, all the way to his initiation into discipleship to Jesus Christ. Evangelism that is personal involves going and joining people on their journey to Jesus. Evangelism that is personal involves going with beloved children, forgetters, and outsiders all the way to their baptism (or renewal of their baptismal vows); journeying with them all the way through their initiation into discipleship to Jesus Christ.

Discipleship to Jesus is the goal of our evangelism. Evangelism is the means to the end of helping people become followers of Jesus who are united to Jesus by faith and live lives of joyful obedience to him, participating in God's redemptive mission in the world. Evangelism that is personal involves journeying with people to that end. Like Philip, the Holy Spirit is speaking to each one of us, saying, "Get up in the chariot and go with people on their journey to Jesus."

Journeying with people is Jesus's method of evangelism. Jesus invests the final three years of his life walking roads, taking sea voyages, worshiping in synagogues and in the temple, and lodging overnight with a select group of men and women. He laughs with them, weeps with them, teaches them, learns from them, and shares life with them. In the villages of Galilee, the cities of Decapolis, and the Judean wilderness, his disciples are constantly by his side. His method of initiating people into discipleship to himself is intensely personal. He is with his disciples, and, through their association with him, these men and women take on his habits, teachings, and characteristics, ultimately putting their faith in him. In his classic book *The Master Plan of Evangelism*, Robert Coleman writes, "[Jesus] actually spent more time with his disciples than with everybody else in the world put together."[1]

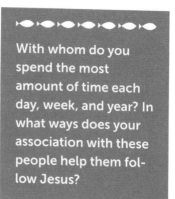

With whom do you spend the most amount of time each day, week, and year? In what ways does your association with these people help them follow Jesus?

We learn from Jesus that evangelism that is personal involves an investment of your personal time and takes a long time. This is true whether we are initiating our beloved children, forgetters, or outsiders into discipleship to Jesus. And it is true for almost every person who is a follower of Jesus today.

In 2012, the Vancouver First Church of the Nazarene celebrated its seventy-fifth anniversary. As part of the celebration, the church published a booklet of seventy-five personal stories chronicling how people became followers of Jesus because someone in the church went on a personal journey with them. One of my favorite stories in this booklet is the story of Ken Jarvis's journey to Jesus.

In December 1972, Ken and Marilyn Jarvis purchased the house next door to John and Lena Witte on East 37th Avenue. The Wittes were long time members of the church. Ken was not inclined to go to church, to say the least, but over the years Marilyn participated in a ladies' Bible study often held in the Wittes' home. As they went about their day-to-day lives, John frequently struck up conversations with Ken, often with the simple words, "Hey, neighbor, how ya doin'?" The conversations carried on from there.

The Jarvises and the Wittes shared life together as neighbors sometimes do, and John occasionally invited Ken to church, letting Ken know he would always be welcome. There are many factors, of course, in each person's journey to Jesus. In Ken's case it included the prayers and witness of his wife, Marilyn, the kindness of others whom Ken met from the church, and, most importantly, the work of the Spirit to open his eyes and soften his heart. After many, many years of hearing, "Hey, neighbor, how ya doin'?" from John Witte, Ken found himself drawn into discipleship to Jesus. A step here, a step there—with John walking alongside all the way. In 1995, some twenty-three years after becoming John's neighbor, Ken was initiated into Christian discipleship through repentance and faith in Jesus Christ. John Witte practiced an evangelism that was personal by taking personal interest in his neighbor and remaining personally engaged with him all the way to Jesus.

When we consider going on the journey to Jesus with the beloved children of the church, we sometimes do a great disservice to our young children when we focus on "getting them saved" rather than committing ourselves to go on the journey of lovingly initiating the beloved children of the church into discipleship to Jesus Christ.

A dear Christian woman who calls herself a child evangelist uses a series of colored yarn to gently and lovingly explain to children that God loves them; that they are sinners; that Jesus died for them; and that they need to accept Jesus in order to be saved. She then asks children to raise their hands if they want to accept

Jesus into their hearts. Inevitably, the children do. Every week. Over and over again. The same children "get saved" and ask Jesus into their hearts week after week. I remember adults presenting the gospel to me exactly this same way when I was a child. I remember accepting Jesus into my heart many, many times.

Those who evangelize children this way have good intentions. I appreciate the loving concern of child evangelists. I believe the Spirit of God is at work in the responses of our children to these sorts of presentations—children, who, in childlike faith, open their hearts to Jesus. There are many people today who can remember raising their hands in response to such a question, and identify that moment as the time when their journeys to Jesus began. But I don't want us to think that the work of evangelism, the work of initiating children into discipleship to Jesus, is finished once children ask Jesus into their hearts. And we need to consider whether we might unknowingly confuse the beloved children of our church through these sorts of evangelistic presentations that repeatedly ask them to accept Jesus. Such a practice may cause a child to question why Jesus keeps leaving and has to be asked to come in over and over again.

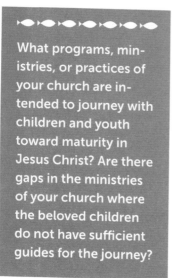

What programs, ministries, or practices of your church are intended to journey with children and youth toward maturity in Jesus Christ? Are there gaps in the ministries of your church where the beloved children do not have sufficient guides for the journey?

In his study of evangelism in the early church, Michael Green finds nothing to suggest that direct evangelizing was ever thought to be necessary for children of believing parents in the early church. "Indeed, the children of believers are already treated as being in the Christian fellowship unless they contract out," Green discovered.

Like the child of a proselyte to Judaism they are regarded as within the covenant unless they determine to cut themselves off from it. It appears that the early Christians took very seriously indeed the words of Jesus asserting that the kingdom of God belonged to children.[2]

Congregations need to develop practices of Christian initiation that value and affirm the special place that our beloved children have among us. It means we invest ourselves in the longer, personal journey of helping our children become mature, adult followers of Jesus, growing into the faith they have received as the inheritance that comes from being part of the community of faith.

Linda came to Vancouver First Church as a three-week-old baby in the arms of her parents, Lorne and Faye. Growing up, VFC was a second home for Linda, a central place for friendship and activity. As the church approached its seventy-fifth anniversary, Linda took time to reflect not only on the rich experiences she enjoyed as a child but also on the church's role in preparing her for a lifetime of following Jesus. She is a maturing follower of Jesus today because of Sunday school teachers, pastors, youth workers, spiritual friends, and mentors who journeyed with her from a childlike trust in Jesus through to a mature faith in Christ.

When we baptize or dedicate children in our churches, pastors often ask the parents and the whole congregation to make a commitment to the children's development as followers of Jesus, asking, "Will you commit yourself as the body of Christ to disciple the children by nurturing their growth toward maturity in Christ?"

The process of leading children toward making personal affirmations of faith and commitments to living as disciples of Jesus was historically known as *catechesis* in the Christian church. Catechesis literally means "to echo." Echoing Jesus must be the goal of the children's and youth programming in the church. But programming does not produce disciples. It is the personal involvement of people as Sunday school teachers, children's church volunteers, friends, mentors, spiritual parents, and brothers and sisters in Christ on the journey that makes disciples.

Consider the beloved children on your high-five prayer list. As you pray for them, look for ways you can go on the journey with them as a mentor, teacher, guide, and friend, helping them become mature followers of Jesus.

We also need to go on the journey to Jesus with forgetters. Forgetters can sometimes be difficult people to go on the journey with. Forgetters have often left the church because of hurt, frustration, or disappointments with people. In such cases it is important to keep the goal of evangelism in mind, and the goal is discipleship to Jesus, not necessarily returning to a particular church or Christian tradition. Discipleship to Jesus involves active participation in the life, mission, and worship of a local church, but for those who have been hurt or wounded by the church, this may take time. On the journey with forgetters, keep discipleship to Jesus as the goal. Jesus is the only one who can heal their hurts. And when forgetters return to Jesus, Jesus will lead them back into a worshiping community.

My friend Shelby was a forgetter. He grew up in a Christian home and was active in the church as a youth. After graduating from high school, he stopped participating in the life and mission of a local church and abandoned discipleship to Jesus. Because of our prior friendship, Shelby connected with me in one of my early pastorates. Shelby had a lot of questions about God and faith. I went on a journey with Shelby, and we began to meet regularly, not only to talk about God but to share life together. He journeyed with me and with the congregation I pastored for a couple of years; then he disappeared. For some people, the journey back to Jesus takes many twists and turns. There were wounds and hurts in Shelby's life that I was not equipped to handle. Some of these hurts were related to an earlier negative experience in a Church of the Nazarene. But I always let Shelby know that I cared about him and that my door was open to him. Shelby and I are Facebook friends now. Much to my surprise, a couple of years ago, he posted on his timeline that he had joined a church from a different ecclesial tradition. I am grateful he has found a church home in another tradition where he can grow and mature as a follower of Jesus. Evangelism that is personal means we go as far on the journey as people will allow us to go, and trust that the Spirit will call others to join forgetters on the journey when we are unable to continue.

Some forgetters leave the journey of discipleship because their hearts are drawn to follow other gods, such as the unholy trinity of money, sex, and power. The truth is, some people who once followed Jesus simply get too busy for God and find discipleship to Jesus to be a hindrance to their personal goals and pursuits. Jesus told us this would happen. It shouldn't surprise us when it does. Some forgetters justify their departure from Jesus by judging and condemning what they see as hypocrisy in the church. These folks can be difficult to be around. But forgetters like these need Christian friends who will stay on the journey with them, even when that journey is unpleasant. We do not know what is going on in the hearts and minds of forgetters. We should not judge them too quickly or harshly. Neither should we assume that just because they were once children of the church, were baptized, or made professions of faith that they are okay. Conversion is the beginning of Christian discipleship, not the end.

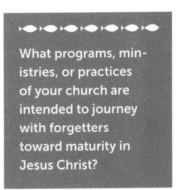

What programs, ministries, or practices of your church are intended to journey with forgetters toward maturity in Jesus Christ?

Evangelism that is personal includes our personal involvement in reviving or recalling those who were once disciples back on the journey to Jesus. Forgetters need to know that their Christian friends and family love them and are willing to go the distance with them. Going the journey with forgetters requires us to remain open to those whose loss of faith may be hurtful to us, to persevere in prayer, to keep our eyes on the horizon, like the father in Luke 15, looking for a sign, something that indicates that the lost son or daughter is starting the journey back home.

We are called to leave our comfortable places and go on similar journeys with outsiders. Outsiders rarely darken the doors of the church. Like Philip in Acts 8, we've got to go to where the outsiders are and join them on their journeys, in their chariots. Journeying to Jesus with outsiders means eating and drinking with sinners, like Jesus. It means letting go of control and allowing someone else to set the agenda instead of forcing others to conform to your timetables. Hospitality is not only inviting people into your home to share your stories; it is accepting an invitation to enter other people's homes and listening to their stories. Outsiders may not even be aware that they are on a spiritual journey. Or, their spiritual journey may not yet be informed by the good news of the gospel. Outsiders may not understand their need for God, or have any comprehension of the blessings of the kingdom of God.

This is the type of guidance Philip offers the Ethiopian eunuch. Starting with where the Ethiopian is, with his questions and inquiries, Philip helps him understand God's big story, how Jesus is the central feature of that story, and how, through faith in Jesus Christ, God seeks to include and enfold him, a Gentile eunuch, into the blessings of the kingdom of God. Of course, the story in Acts 8 makes the journey look very logical and linear. It rarely is.

Amie was an outsider whose journey to Jesus was not logical or linear but was marked throughout by love. Amie's story begins with her neighbor Isabelle, who was a faithful church attender. Amie knew Isabelle for thirty-five years and looked up to her as a woman who had a faith she knew she didn't have.

"I didn't even know what the church was," Amie said to me, "but there was something about the way Isabelle interacted with me that drew me to her. She was staunch, not touchy-feely, but I saw her faith as she went through trials with her kids and grandkids."

When Isabelle lost her driver's license due to age and illness, Amie volunteered to drive her to church. At first she just sat in the parking lot, but Isabelle kept insisting that Amie "just come in." When Amie did come in, she was warmly welcomed by the people in the church. Amie was surprised to learn that she had gone to high school with some of the beloved children of the church.

What programs, ministries, or practices of your church encourage congregants to intentionally go outside the church and journey with outsiders toward maturity in Jesus Christ?

Amie didn't understand much of what was talked about in the sermons when she first started attending. But she made friends who joined her on her journey to Jesus. "Dawn helped me on my personal journey to Jesus," said Amie. "I wanted to be like her. Being with her and the other ladies in the Tuesday night Bible study was amazing."

"Then there was Kadee, the teacher," she said. "I remember at the coffee shop when Kadee asked me if I wanted to invite Jesus into my life and follow him. Nobody had ever asked me that question before. I didn't know where to start, so Kadee suggested I read the gospel of John. She met with me and talked with me and answered questions about what I was reading."

Within a few years, Amie was baptized. She said she wasn't sure about the decision, right up until the morning of her baptism. Then she knew it was what she wanted. Through the companionship of Dawn, Kadee, Isabelle, and others, Amie has become a follower of Jesus.

Now Amie is joining others on their journey to Jesus. Her daughter, her long-time neighbor, and new friends are among those Amie journeys with. She prays for her family and friends to know and follow Jesus. She simply shares what she knows and opens her life to people. Amie practices an evangelism that is personal. She is an informal evangelist. She simply loves Jesus and is excited for others to discover the one who has found her.

Most Christians believe they should be involved in evangelism, but few people actually report doing so. The research shows that many people are not interested or willing to be involved in evangelism. But I've come to discover that's not true. Sure, Christians don't want to be involved in evangelism that is *impersonal:* knocking on people's doors; standing on a street corner handing out tracts; buttonholing people at work; or memorizing presentations of the gospel that rely on logic, argumentation, and rhetorical techniques to pressure people into agreeing with one's views. But most Christians are *willing* to and *do* pray personally for the people they know and love to become followers of Jesus; they are *willing* to and *do* share personal stories about Jesus with the people they know and love; they are *willing* to and *do* go on personal journeys with the people they know and love. Most Christians, at least the ones I've had the privilege of pastoring, want to help guide people to Jesus. The church, all of us together, exists to help and encourage one another on that mission. Evangelism is the heart of our mission. When we are engaged in this good work, we come alive!

Evangelism that is personal *does* require intent. It is easy to neglect this aspect of our mission. Maybe we just need to be reminded to keep on doing the personal work of loving people into the kingdom of God through our prayers, sharing personal stories, and going on journeys with people. When we remember how *we* became followers of Jesus—as beloved children who were loved into faith by our friends, family, and a congregation; as forgetters who were not forgotten by friends, family, and a congregation; as outsiders who were welcomed, guided, and loved by friends, family, and a congregation—this will spur us on to engage in practices of evangelism that are personal. It is for the love of God and others that we remain faithful to this good work. And it is by the power of the Spirit that we bear the good fruit of the kingdom of God.

All throughout the Scriptures we see that God is actively fulfilling God's purpose to draw people from every tongue, tribe, and nation into God's divine life; lovingly and intentionally drawing people who are near and far into fellowship with the Father, through the Son, by the Spirit. And we also see how God sends people as witnesses into the wide and wondrous world to join others on their journey to Jesus. God makes disciples through disciples. God makes disciples through ordinary people like Philip, John Witte, Isabelle, and Amie. Ordinary people like you and me. God makes disciples through followers of Jesus who are willing and available to go with others on their journey to Jesus, whether they are our beloved children, forgetters, or outsiders like the Ethiopian eunuch. God makes disciples through people who start wherever their children, friends, family members, neighbors, or colleagues are and go the distance with them—even if that starting place is a highway through the Gaza Strip. Go with people on their journey to Jesus. This is evangelism that is personal.

Notes

Introduction

1. Chilcote and Warner, *The Study of Evangelism*, xxvi-xxvii. Propositions 1, 2, 3, 4, 5, and 7 are directly attributable to Chilcote and Warner; however, I present them in a different order.

Chapter 1

1. Thomas G. Long, *The Witness Of Preaching, Second Edition*, 2nd ed. (Westminster John Knox Press, 2005), 47.
2. Michael W. Goheen, *A Light to the Nations: The Missional Church and the Biblical Story* (Baker Academic, 2011), 37.
3. Ibid., 39.
4. Randy L Maddox, *Responsible Grace: John Wesley's Practical Theology* (Nashville, Tenn: Kingswood Books, 1994), 111.
5. Ibid.
6. Ibid., 112–113.
7. Walter Brueggemann, *Biblical Perspectives on Evangelism: Living in a Three-Storied Universe* (Abingdon Press, 1993), 71. The language of *constituents of our witness*; *beloved children*; *forgetters*; and *outsiders* is taken from this book.
8. Walter Brueggemann, *The Prophetic Imagination* (Philadelphia: Fortress Press, 1978), 71.

Chapter 2

1. Bob McDonald, "The Science of Religion," *Quirks & Quarks with Bob McDonald*, accessed May 4, 2013, http://www.cbc.ca/quirks/episode/2013/03/30/march-30-2013/#3.
2. Ibid.
3. Marva J. Dawn, *A Royal Waste of Time: The Splendor of Worshiping God and Being Church for the World* (William B. Eerdmans Publishing Company, 1999), 113.
4. This paragraph, and the use of Psalm 96, were inspired by Christopher Wright's book *The Mission of God's People: A Biblical Theology of the Church's Mission* (Zondervan, 2010), 244-262.
5. John Dickson, *The Best Kept Secret of Christian Mission: Promoting the Gospel with More Than Our Lips* (Zondervan, 2010), 170–171.

6. Ibid., 171.

7. Ibid., 166.

8. "Two Thirds of Adults Formerly in Church Would Consider Returning | LifeWay Research," accessed May 6, 2013, http://www.lifeway.com/ArticleView?storeId=10054&catalogId=10001&langId=-1&article=LifeWay-Research-surveys-formerly-churched-part-2-of-2.

9. Haldor Lillenas, "Wonderful Grace of Jesus," *Sing to the Lord* (Lillenas Publishing Co., 1993), hymn #360.

10. Ben Fielding and Reuben Morgan, "Mighty to Save," *Mighty to Save* (Hillsong Publishing, 2006), track #14.

11. Marva J. Dawn, *A Royal Waste of Time*, 69.

12. Paul W. Chilcote, "The Integral Nature of Worship and Evangelism," in *The Study of Evangelism: Exploring a Missional Practice of the Church*, ed. Paul W. Chilcote and Laceye C. Warner (Wm. B. Eerdmans Publishing Company, 2008), 262.

13. Ibid., 263.

14. Eugene H. Peterson, *The Jesus Way: A Conversation on the Ways That Jesus Is the Way*, First (William B. Eerdmans Publishing Company, 2007), 5-6.

Chapter 3

1. Benji Rodes, *The Fire Reply*, 2013, 11.

2. Ibid., 29.

3. Ibid., 34.

4. Ibid., 41.

5. Ibid., 88.

6. Thomas G. Long, *Matthew*, 1st ed. (Westminster John Knox Press, 1997), 19.

7. James M. Houston, *The Transforming Friendship: A Guide to Prayer* (Oxford: Lion Publishing, 1991), 6.

8. Ibid., 7.

Chapter 4

1. Christopher J. H. Wright, *The Mission of God's People: A Biblical Theology of the Church's Mission* (Zondervan, 2010), 122 & 126.

2. Bryan P. Stone, *Evangelism after Christendom: The Theology and Practice of Christian Witness* (Brazos Press, 2007), 15.

3. Michael Green, *Evangelism in the Early Church* (Hodder & Stoughton, 1970), xv.

4. Rodney Stark, *The Triumph of Christianity: How the Jesus Movement Became the World's Largest Religion*, Reprint (HarperOne, 2012), 106–112.

5. Ibid., 112.

6. Dickson, *The Best Kept Secret of Christian Mission*, 92.

7. Ibid.

8. Ibid., 93.

9. Green, *Evangelism in the Early Church*, xvi.

10. Stan Ingersol, *Nazarene Roots: Pastors, Prophets, Revivalists & Reformers* (Beacon Hill Press of Kansas City, 2009), 89.

11. Ibid., 89–90.

12. Harold Ivan Smith, *Quotable Bresee, The* (Beacon Hill, 1983), 168.

13. Wright, *The Mission of God's People*, 94–95.

Chapter 5

1. "Victory in Europe Day," *Wikipedia, the Free Encyclopedia*, May 24, 2013, http://en.wikipedia.org/w/index.php?title=Victory_in_Europe_Day&oldid=554950126.

2. Scott J Jones, *The Evangelistic Love of God and Neighbor: A Theology of Witness and Discipleship* (Abingdon Press, 2003), 33.

3. In *The Evangelistic Love of God and Neighbor,* Jones, who builds on the work of William Abraham, provides the following definition of evangelism: "Evangelism is that set of loving, intentional activities governed by the goal of initiating persons into Christian discipleship in response to the reign of God" (18).

Chapter 6

1. Barna Group, "Is Evangelism Going Out of Style?," accessed December 19, 2013, https://www.barna.org/barna-update/faith-spirituality/648-is-evangelism-going-out-of-style#.UrJjtuLhFnk.

2. Dickson, *The Best Kept Secret of Christian Mission*, 75.

Chapter 7

1. Dickson, *The Best Kept Secret of Christian Mission*, 143.

2. Green, *Evangelism in the Early Church*, 211.

3. William J Abraham, *The Art of Evangelism: Evangelism Carefully Crafted into the Life of the Local Church* (Eugene: Wipf & Stock Publishers, 2011), 47.

4. Ibid.

5. Thomas G. Long, *Testimony: Talking Ourselves into Being Christian*, 1st ed. (Jossey-Bass, 2004), 5.

6. See Scot McKnight, *The King Jesus Gospel: The Original Good News Revisited* (Zondervan, 2011), 133.

Chapter 8

1. Robert Coleman, *The Master Plan of Evangelism* (Grand Rapids, Mich.: F.H. Revell, 1993), 41–50.

2. Michael Green, *Evangelism in the Early Church*, Updated (Eagle, Guildford, 1995), 266.